世界のシニアリビング
Retiring in Style
Around the WORLD

Edited by
Masuhiro Agari

序文
Foreword

Designing for Seniors
　- maximizing the possibilities for a full life

As I was preparing my thoughts for this foreword, it occurred to me that it was approximately thirty years ago that I began my career with senior living facilities. During the 1970's in the U.S., new HUD programs for the elderly emerged. These programs served the dual purpose of providing housing for lower-income elderly as well as highlighting for private, developers the need and growing market for all forms of housing and facilities for this impending age group. Historically, of course, there were "old folk's homes", sponsored by governments, veterans' groups, religious denominations and other not-for-profit, benevolent organizations. However these facilities were few in number and lean on thoughtful design.

With the increase in the number of seniors in Europe, Japan and the United States, much has evolved over the intervening years in architecture for the aging. The projects we see today are greatly different, much more varied and more responsive to the needs and pleasures of the population served. The evolution - and the increased sophistication - of the Continuing Care Retirement Community (CCRC), with its integrated levels of care and services blended in a cohesive "campus" offer greater diversity, balance, choice, and care than ever before possible to retirees. Yet, I believe, underlying this evolution are the same well-grounded design goals that challenged us thirty years ago and discussed below. The aim of the architect in serving our elderly populations remains the achievement of this set of goals. Achieving them makes this building type unique.....and therein resides the rewards of designing facilities for this important age group.

The goals spring from an understanding of the needs of seniors, but also from the capabilities and joys and diverse interests that characterize them as a group. Remembering that they are as varied and wide-ranging in their likes/dislikes, entertainments, backgrounds and interests as your own age-sector is the first step in serving them well. The

高齢者のための住まい
　- 充実した時の流れる場所

この序文を書きながら、私が30年程前にシニアリビング施設の設計に携わり始めた頃のことを思い起こす。1970年代、米国では高齢者のための新しい住宅・都市政策の展開が盛んな頃であった。この政策によって、所得水準の低い高齢者のために居住施設が整備されたと同時に、デベロッパーには高齢化する世代のためのさまざまな形式の高齢者施設の市場の拡大という状況がが訪れた。しかしそこに至るまでに、政府や復員軍人のグループ、宗教団体、その他の非営利団体による「従来型の民間ホーム」はあったにせよ、その数は少なく配慮の行き届いた設計であったとは言い難い。

ヨーロッパや米国、日本での高齢者数の増加とともに、その建築のあり様も変化し、今日では居住者のさまざまな要求に応じたそこでの生活を楽しめるものへと様変わりした。この「キャンパス」での多様な介護やサービスなどの組み合わせによって、終身介護施設(CCRC = Continuing Care Retirement Community)が新たな機能を複合化させながら進化することで、居住者はかつてなかったほどの多様性やバランス、選択性、介護を享受することができる。とはいえ、この進化がめざすところは、30年前からあった設計のゴールと少しも変わりがないと言える。高齢者に仕える建築家の目標は、彼等の目的の達成を補助することでもある。このことが高齢者施設を特異なものとしているが、そこにこの種の建築を設計することの喜びがある。

高齢者のニーズを理解することで設計の目標を設定することができるが、彼等の身体能力や楽しみ、趣味などにも注目することが大切である。それには幅広い嗜好や娯楽、生い立ち、興味を知ることから始め、建築が彼等にとって優れた生活の場のひとつとなるべきであることを建築家は自覚しなければならない。そこで

second key acknowledgment of the designer is to remember that while architecture is critical, it is only one of several components in creating a successful living place for seniors. Architecture must weave with and support the programs, services and "community" that embrace the residents in their daily lives. Retirement communities are not real estate alone, they are not architecture alone, rather they are a distinctive blend of architectural design with the social, spiritual, cultural and supportive components of a care giving community.

So, then, how does the architect best approach this project type? How best can the architect serve this special user? For some time now, the planning of a retirement community has been guided by the principle that a home, rather than an institution, should be created, to the unfortunate extent that the principle is too often a cliché. While recognition of this point represents a huge advance over earlier conceptions of care for the aged, its cliché quality is due to the fact that it is easier to state than to deliver. It is only recently that the combined talents of designers, sponsors, specialists in aging and social scientists have been directed to the task of translating the principle into bricks and mortar.

The first more-specific guiding principle is based on the questions, "Homelike for whom?" Each of us has a tendency to project our own values and preferences into our ideas about what is "right" for others. The result is often a product or building that fails hugely in meeting the needs of those with different preferences. Obviously, then, a major component of the design of a retirement community must be the wishes of those for whom it is designed. Although seniors are capable of expressing much more about those wishes than they are sometimes given the opportunity to convey, they suffer - as all of us do - from a lack of complete awareness about how their environment influences them. Therefore, in addition to asking the seniors what they wish, it is necessary to know how they actually use their environment, and to be ready to apply knowledge about the aging process to physical design solutions. This approach will maximize the possibility of a full life in ways

は居住者等の日常生活が繰り広げられる「コミュニティ」やプログラム、サービスが上手く働くような建築のあり方が求められている。高齢者コミュニティとは単なる敷地や建物のことではなく、そこでの交流や精神的・文化的な要素、運営設備・体制などが程よく反映された建築デザインによって生ずるものである。

では、建築家はこの種のプロジェクトにどのようにアプローチすることができるのだろうか。また、このように特殊なユーザーに最善を尽すにはどうすればよいのだろうか。最近の高齢者施設の計画では、「施設」というよりも「家」が創られるべきであるという原則が支配的である。このことは高齢者施設が作られ始めた時期のコンセプトよりはるかに優れているにせよ、その言葉の響きの良さのあまり、軽々しく頻繁に言われすぎてきたことは否めない。実際に行うことは単に言うより難しである。事実、最近になってやっと建築家と事業者、そして高齢化や社会科学の専門家のチームによって、この原則が建築へと具現化され始めた。

その原則は、「誰のための家なのか」という疑問を持つことで具体性をおびてくる。人は自分の価値観に基づいて、自分にとって「良いこと」は他人にとっても「良いこと」と思いがちである。製品や建物などの場合、これでは異なる嗜好性を持つ他人のニーズに叶うことはできない。高齢者コミュニティの設計では、潜在的入居者の希望を取り入れることが重要である。機会さえ与えられれば、高齢者は自分の希望の多くを表現し伝えることができるが、生活環境がいかに彼等に影響を及ぼすかについての意識を、我々同様、完全に欠如している。従って、彼等の希望に耳を傾けることに加えて、彼等が置かれた環境をどのように使うのかを知ることや、加齢の進行に関する知識を設計に適用することが必要である。このアプローチによってそこでの生活は、その意識を超えて充実したものとなる。彼等が必要とすることや能力は加齢とともに変化するの

that may be beyond the awareness of the user. The fact is that needs and capabilities do sometimes change with age, and planning/design must achieve the proper balance between encouraging the continuation of life styles while taking account of age changes. The goal is to facilitate this continuity whilst compensating for negative changes.

The core needs -the "well-grounded design goals" mentioned earlier- that a total CCRC should fulfill include the following:
• Independence - This is the most highly-valued of all needs. The older person who can see herself making maximum use of her capabilities will preserve her self-esteem. Doing for oneself is always preferable to a dependent state; proper planning can enhance independence in countless ways. Good and thoughtful design can enhance and prolong independence; thoughtless or absent design can present obstacles to it.
• Security - Every person has a limit to his or her full independence and is able to accept these limitations. Safe environments are important for all of us in terms of avoiding accidents, protection from intruders, and knowledge that help is available when needed. The greater vulnerability of many seniors requires that high priority be given to security: CCRC location, site planning, building design (orientation, overviews as well as responsive detailing and material selections), all contribute to security.
• Social integration - The sense of being connected to others - whether as giver or receiver - or even in casual terms, is a basic need for everyone. Physical planning and design can support or obstruct the possibility for fulfilling social needs and must consider every design decision in terms of its potential impact on social behavior.
• Privacy - We have equally strong needs for being able to choose to be alone, to have our own unique territory, to be able to do as we wish or express our individuality without intrusion by others. The "institution" concept negates such needs; the "home" concept allows their fulfillment without frustrating the need for social togetherness.
• Satisfying uses of time - Society removes many of the

で、建築計画や設計ではライフスタイルの変化と加齢による変化との適切なバランスを達成すべきであり、ネガティブな変化を補いながら生活の持続性を促進することがゴールとなる。

優れたCCRCは次のようなニーズに応じている。
・自立性 - 最も尊ばれるべきニーズ。健康な高齢者は自分の尊厳を保とうとする。人に頼らずに身の回りのことができるのは常に望ましいことである。この自立性は、適切な建築計画によって際限なく増強されることができる。配慮ある優れたデザインもまた長期にわたってこの自立性に資するが、そうでない場合はこの逆となる。
・安全 - 人は完全な自立性を保ちつづけることには限界があり、またそのことを受け入れることができる。事故に遭わないようにし、侵入者から身を守り、必要な時に助けを呼べるという意味での安全な環境が必要となる。ある意味で弱者である高齢者は、安全性を優先度の高いものと考えている。そのためにCCRCの立地やその配置計画、建物デザイン（向き、眺望、適切なディテールと材料の使用）が考慮されるべきである。
・交流 - その目的のいかんに拠らず、人は他人との交流を求める。この交流は、建築デザインの良し悪しによって促進もされるし阻害もされる。従って良い建築デザインが交流のきっかけとなることを忘れてはならない。
・プライバシー - 人は誰でも一人で居たいと願うことや、自分の好きなテリトリーを築きたいと思うこと、他人から邪魔されずに個性を保ちそれを発揮したいという願望を一様にもっている。「施設」ではこのようなニーズを無視するが、「家」は社会との接点を保ちつつもそのニーズに叶うものである。

vehicles that make activities meaningful for the elderly person. An essential element in the planning process is to provide a wide variety of choices for the resident in pursuing former interests or developing new ones. Choice - the maximization of choice - can be seen as the central aspiration for the majority of design decisions in the retirement community.

• Maintaining linkages to the wider community - A sense of living is conveyed through access to family, friends, shopping, entertainment and culture outside of the retirement community. Design and operations need to ensure the accessibility and comfortable enticement of the retirement community to outsiders and of the outside community to the residents.

• A sense of pride in one's environment - Beauty, in both natural and man-made surroundings, conveys to the resident a feeling of personal worth and social pride. Access to nature provides important connections to the cycle of life for the resident and staff.

The planning and design of the projects that follow incorporate many of these principles in their execution. When studying the excellent case studies collected in this book, give thought to these principles and the application of design on those principles that have helped to create the projects presented. My own thinking over these many years about this fulfilling project-type was guided early-on by a pioneer in the study of aging and seniors, Dr. Powell Lawton of the Philadelphia Geriatric Center. His studious and sensitive thoughts about seniors have aided me throughout my numerous projects and are reflected in the points I have made above.

Dennis Cope, AIA
President
Office of Dennis Cope/Architect

・有意義な時間 - 高齢者のアクティビティをより充実したものとする多くの機会が、社会から欠落している。居住者がこれまでの嗜好を深めたり新たなものに興味を抱いたりできるような選択の幅とその拡張を意識しながら建築計画を行うことが欠かせない。

・地域社会とのつながり - 人が生活するということには、家族や友人とのふれあいやショッピング、高齢者コミュニティの外での娯楽や文化などが含まれている。高齢者コミュニティとその外部のコミュニティとが相互に行き来できることが、設計や運営に求められる。

・その場での尊厳 - 自然物であろうが人工物であろうがそれらが美しければ、人はそれらを通して自分の価値に気付き社会での誇りを感じることができる。特に、居住者やスタッフの周りに自然があることが大切である。

本書で取りあげているプロジェクトには、実際にこれらの原則が適用されている。それらの優れた事例を通して、プロジェクトごとの原則に対する姿勢や、それに基づくデザインの展開を知ることができる。さまざまな要素が絡み合うこの種のプロジェクトに対する私の姿勢は、加齢と高齢者に関する分野での研究のパイオニアである、フィラデルフィアの老人センターのポウェル・ロウトン博士の教えによるものである。これまで私が係わってきたプロジェクトの多くは、博士の研究とその成果が背景にあり、本序文に寄せても同様である。

デニス・コープ
米国建築家協会会員
オフィス・オブ・デニス・コープ / アーキテクト代表

目次
Table of Contents

002 序文
Foreword

第 1 章　Chapter One
都市機能と生活支援機能を連携させた

拡張型
Extending Program

010　クラシックレジデンス・ハイアット・パロアルト
　　　Classic Residence by Hyatt, Palo Alto

018　サンシティ町田 - CCRC
　　　Sun City Machida - CCRC

024　サンシティ町田
　　　Sun City Machida

030　エレガーノ摩耶・フォセッタ摩耶
　　　Elegano Maya Fosseta Maya

036　リバーランディング・サンディリッジ
　　　River Landing at Sandy Ridge

042　グリューネスハイム新山手
　　　Grünes Heim Shinyamanote

046　ペニンシュラ・リージェント
　　　Peninsula Regent

050　ウィルマーク香椎浜
　　　Will Mark Kashiihama

第 2 章　Chapter Two
既存施設の機能を高レベルで強化した

リノベーション型
Strategic Repositioning

058　ブリッジポイント・アシステッドリビング
　　　Bridgepoint Assisted Living

064　サンシティ熊谷 - CCRC
　　　Sun City Kumagaya - CCRC

070　エセックス＆サセックスホテル
　　　Essex & Sussex Hotel

076　サクラビア成城
　　　Sacravia Seijo

082　ザ・トラディション・パームビーチ
　　　The Tradition of the Palm Beaches

086　ギヴンズ・エステート
　　　Givens Estates

090　エルダーズゲート終身介護施設
　　　Aldersgate Continuing Care Retirement Community

第3章　Chapter Three
地域性への配慮にこだわった
地域密着型
Reflected Locality

096　マラヴィラ
　　　Maravilla

102　サンシティ横浜
　　　Sun City Yokohama

108　カールスバッド・バイ・ザ・シー
　　　Carlsbad by the Sea

114　ディアージュ神戸
　　　Diage Kobe

120　ツインレークス・モンゴメリー
　　　Twin Lakes at Montgomery

126　シニオレンハウス・セントニコラス
　　　Seniorenhaus St. Nikolaus

132　ザ・アトリウム・シダース・リタイアメントコミュニティ
　　　The Atrium at Cedars Retirement Community

138　サンシティ神奈川 - ケアセンター
　　　Sun City Kanagawa - Care Center

140　ロイヤルライフ多摩
　　　Royal Life Tama

146　ザ・ハミルトン
　　　The Hamilton

152　シーショアガーデンズ・リビングセンター
　　　Seashore Gardens Living Center

158　エレガーノ甲南
　　　Elegano Konan

162　ニューベリーコート・リタイアメントコミュニティ
　　　Newbury Court Retirement Community

	ゲリアトリック・ナーシングホーム
168	Geriatric Nursing Home

	グランダ夙川
174	Granda Syukugawa

	サンシティ宝塚
176	Sun City Takarazuka

	バッキンガムズ・チョイス
182	Buckingham's Choice

第4章　Chapter Four
大都市での利便性に恵まれた
都心回帰型
Tokyo Experiment

	ザ・バーリントンハウス馬事公苑
186	The Barrington House Bajikoen

	アリア恵比寿
192	Aria Ebisu

	アリア馬事公苑
196	Aria Bajikoen

	コムスンガーデン桜新町
198	Comsn Garden Sakurashinmachi

	コムスンガーデン用賀の杜
199	Comsn Garden Yoganomori

	チャーミングスクエア白金
200	Charming Square Shirogane

	サンシティ銀座・イースト
202	Sun City Ginza East

	謝辞
205	Acknowledgments

	照会先
207	References

第一章
都市機能と生活支援機能を連携させた
拡張型

Chapter One
***Extended
Program***

Classic Residence by Hyatt, Palo Alto

クラシックレジデンス・ハイアット・パロアルト

スタンフォード大学が提供するプログラムと連携するCCRC
Full service CCRC built adjacent to Stanford University that offers a full range of aging in place options.

ウォーターガーデン越しに見るフォーマル・ダイニングルーム（写真：ベニー・チャン、フォトワークス）
View of formal dining room across water garden (photo: Benny Chan, Fotoworks)

スタインバーグ・アーキテクツの設計によるこのクラシックレジデンスのプロジェクトは、街のさまざまな利便施設に近接する「その場所で年を重ねることができる」高齢者施設である。90,000平方メートルの敷地に展開する延べ床面積93,000平方メートルのこの施設は、健常者ユニットや介護ユニット、養護ユニットなどの施設群からなる、ハイアット・コーポレーションによるフラッグシップ・プロジェクトである。クラシックレジデンスは、敷地に近接する文化・医療サービス、さまざまな広さや形のユニット、コミュニティ活動への意識や参加を促すような空間計画が特徴となっている。

クラシックレジデンスの建築計画では、高齢者特有のニーズに応じながら、敷地の持つさまざまな制約を解決している。各居住者のレベルに応じたアクティビティや交流の促進を意識する一方、既存のカリフォルニアオークや近くの入江、この地方のクラフトマンスタイルの建築様式に配慮した形状の建物となっている。全ての建築的要素には、オーガニックな色彩や素材、意匠が用いられている。木材やスタッコ、露出した構造、地域の石材、装飾窓などの全てが、この地方のクラフトマンシップを反映し、屋内外での快適な環境を創るという設計意図を具現化するのに役立っている。

5,600平方メートルもの共用部には、フォーマル・ダイニングやインフォーマル・ダイニング、屋内外のカフェ(3つのレストラン)、総合ビジネスセンター、ライブラリー、シアター、多目的ルーム、フィットネスセンター、プール、ストア、デイスパなどの施設がある。ここでは、各種の機能が複合化する高齢者居住施設の昨今の顕著な傾向を反映するばかりか、近隣の大学や病院、高級ショッピングモールをもその機能に加えている。

表玄関と車寄せ（写真：ベニー・チャン、フォトワークス）
Main entrance and porte-cochere (photo: Benny Chan, Fotoworks)

By providing a variety of health service levels in close proximity to a variety of community resources, the Classic Residence project by Steinberg Architects offers a unique aging-in-place option for seniors. Totaling nearly one million square feet over 22 acres, this flagship project by the Hyatt Corporation provides independent living units, assisted living units and a skilled nursing facility in three distinct, yet unified buildings. Overall, Classic Residence capitalizes on adjacent cultural and medical services, a varied range of unit types, sizes and configurations and spatial planning to stimulate interest and involvement in the community.

Planning of the Classic Residence project evolved directly from the specialized needs of seniors and sensitive existing site conditions: clustered activities cater to the activity levels of each group and focus on increased socialization, while building configurations respond to existing specimen California Oaks, an adjacent creek, and regional Craftsman style architecture. All architectural elements on site are tied together through an organic palette of colors, materials and styling. Wood, stucco, expressed structural members, local stone and ornamental windows all respond to the local Craftsman influence and support the design goals to blend with the environment in a relaxed, indoor-outdoor atmosphere.

Highlights of the facility include a 60,000 square foot common area with formal and informal dining, an indoor-outdoor cafe (three restaurants in total), full business center, library, theater, multipurpose space, fitness and aquatic center, general store and day spa. The project supports a growing trend among senior living facilities of utilizing the resources of a mixed-use facility: joint use with universities, hospitals and in this case, a high-end shopping mall.

Client: Classic Residence by Hyatt
Architect: Steinberg Architects
    (Principal-In-Charge: William Williams, AIA)
    (Design Principal: Robert Steinberg, FAIA)
    (Project Designer: Hong Chen, AIA)
    (Project Manager: Dennis Cook, AIA)
Interior Designer: Wilson & Associates
Landscape Designer: The SWA Group
Predominant Contractor: Devcon Construction, Inc.

介護施設の眺め（写真：ベニー・チャン、フォトワークス）
View of assisted living facility (photo: Benny Chan, Fotoworks)

インフォーマル・ダイニングホールのトレリス（写真：ベニー・チャン、フォトワークス）
Outdoor trellised area outside informal dining hall (photo: Benny Chan, Fotoworks)

Location: Stanford, CA U.S.A.
Completion: 2005
Site Area: 90,700 sqm
Gross Floor Area: 93,000 + sqm
Height: Under ground 1 story; Above ground 4 stories
Structure: Concrete structure
Number of Rooms: 388 rooms
Parking: 523 cars
Finishes:
<Predominant Exterior Wall>
	Stone and Plaster
<Main lobby>
	Floor: Stone, Wood, Carpet
	Wall: Wood Paneling
	Ceiling: Wood Paneling
Award:
2006 Grand Award, Pacific Coast Builders Conference/Builder Magazine, Best Attached Senior Housing Project
2005 Gold and Silver Awards, NAHB Best of Senior Housing Design Awards, Large Continuing Care Retirement Community
2005 Best of California Award, McGraw Hill
2004 Gold Award, NAHB Best of Senior Housing Design Awards - On the Boards, Large Continuing Care Retirement Community

中庭から見る介護棟（写真：ベニー・チャン、フォトワークス）
View of Care building from courtyard (photo: Benny Chan, Fotoworks)

スタンフォード大学の所有地を借りたこのハイアットのプロジェクトでは、快適な生活の持続性と多様なサービスを提供しつつ、コミュニティの感覚を創り出すことが課題であった。中庭の周りには388室のユニットが配されている。5,600平方メートルの共用部には、ダイニングやビジネスセンター、ライブラリー、多目的スペース、管理事務所がある。3階建てのヘルスセンターには、70室の介護ユニットと59床の養護施設があり、「その場所で年を重ねることができる」というニーズに応えている。

Providing a continuum of living arrangements and variety of services together while creating a strong sense of community was a major design challenge on this site owned by Stanford University and leased by Hyatt. The project contains 388 units built around a series of courtyards. A 60,000 square foot common facility incorporates dining, business center, library, multipurpose space, and administrative center. A 3-story health center with 70 assisted living units and a 59-bed skilled nursing facility provide aging in place options.

ライブラリー（写真：スタインバーグ・アーキテクツ）
Library (photo: Steinberg Architects)

ロビー（暖炉を見る）（写真：スタインバーグ・アーキテクツ）
Lobby (view to fireplace) (photo: Steinberg Architects)

エレベータ・ロビー（写真：スタインバーグ・アーキテクツ）
Elevator Lobby (photo: Steinberg Architects)

ロビーの廊下（写真：スタインバーグ・アーキテクツ）
Lobby hallway (photo: Steinberg Architects)

アクティビィルーム・多目的室（写真：スタインバーグ・アーキテクツ）
Activity Room/Multipurpose Room (photo: Steinberg Architects)

ダイニング・ウィングの廊下（写真：スタインバーグ・アーキテクツ）
Dining wing hallway (photo: Steinberg Architects)

アートスタジオ（写真：スタインバーグ・アーキテクツ）
Art Studio (photo: Steinberg Architects)

Classic Residence by Hyatt, Palo Alto 015

居室の廊下（写真：スタインバーグ・アーキテクツ）
Residential corridor (photo: Steinberg Architects)

介護棟共用部（写真：ベニー・チャン、フォトワークス）
Public area of Care building (photo: Benny Chan, Fotoworks)

マスタープラン
Master plan

配置図
Site plan

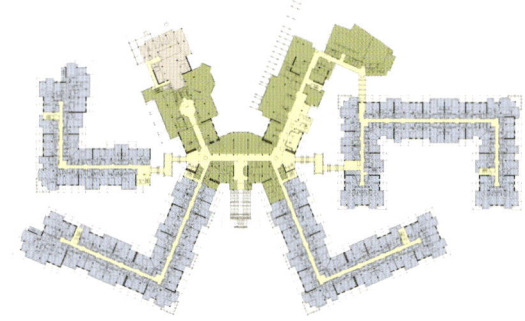
健常棟平面図
Independent Living building plan

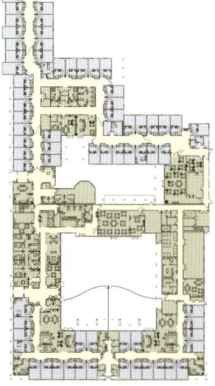
介護棟平面図
Care facility plan

居室平面図
Unit plan

ガゼボー（写真：ベニー・チャン、フォトワークス）
Gazebo (photo: Benny Chan, Fotoworks)

庭から見る居住ウィング（写真：ベニー・チャン、フォトワークス）
View of residential wing from sensory garden (photo: Benny Chan, Fotoworks)

中庭とウォーターガーデン（写真：ベニー・チャン、フォトワークス）
View of back courtyard and water garden (photo: Benny Chan, Fotoworks)

Classic Residence by Hyatt, Palo Alto 017

Sun City Machida - CCRC

サンシティ町田 - CCRC

健常棟と介護棟が共用部で結ばれた丘の上のキャンパス
A CCRC composed of two buildings linked by a common L2 Public Level. "Plaza Building" is skilled nursing/assisted living; "Tower Building" is independent living apartments.

読書やゲーム、展示に使われるライブラリー（写真：小林浩志）
The CCRC library is used for reading, games, gallery exhibits, etc. (photo: Koji Kobayashi)

サンシティ町田は、「タワー棟」（8階建ての健常棟）と「プラザ棟」（5階建てのスキルドナーシング・認知症・介護住居棟）とが、2階の共用部で結ばれている終身介護施設である。

区域内にある既存の病院を含みながら、景観の連続性や調和、コミュニティの感覚を創出することで、異なる用途の建築群からなるキャンパスを丘の上に創ろうとした。敷地の特性から、遠くから見栄えのするこのキャンパスには屋外にさまざまの場があり、外出が難しい要介護者や要養護者と自然との係わりに配慮している。また、健常棟の全居室が東や南西に向いていることで居住性を高めている（このことは日本では重視されている）。

自然環境を最大限に享受することや、快適性や自立性、安全性、多様性に配慮しながら全てのレベルでの生活に選択の幅を広げること、丁寧な「おもてなし」の意識をもって居住者の日常に接するコミュニティをつくること、などが共同設計チームのデザインポリシーであった。運営スタッフと設計チームの緊密な協働によってホスピタリティのイメージと「西洋」での高齢者居住のためのアメニティとが上手く組み合わされた。日米の審美感の融合した建物では、ペット飼育や屋内・屋外園芸などの活動ができる等、斬新な介護哲学が具現化されている。

Sun City Machida is a CCRC composed of two buildings linked by a common L2 public level: the "Tower Building" (8 1/2 stories of independent living) and the "Plaza Building" (5 stories of skilled nursing, dementia and assisted living).

The site-planning concept was to create a "hilltop campus of buildings"; a campus that accommodates the unique requirements of each senior living building type - including an existing hospital - while providing continuity, harmony and a sense of community. The campus, through the site relationships of its buildings, creates a series of protected outdoor rooms, frames important long-distance views, provides a link with Nature (especially for those AL and SN residents who have limited outdoor access), and addresses the Client's requirement that all independent living apartments have either an east or south-southwest orientation (the most culturally-preferred orientations in Japan). The design philosophy developed by the collaborative team of designers (architectural, landscape, interior and art) was to weave a community that: provides maximum passive and active access to Nature, encourages aging-in-place, promotes independence/security/diversity at all living levels by providing maximum choice, and celebrates the cultural respect of these residents with an invigorating, dignified, "hospitality" environment. The Client directive to create a hospitality image and incorporate "western" senior lifestyle amenities formed a close collaboration between the operating staff and design team. The resulting designs that emerged are a blend of eastern and western esthetics, and they introduced new care-giving philosophies - such as pets and indoor/outdoor gardening - to this operator of senior living facilities.

2層分の吹き抜けのあるタワー棟のロビー（写真：松岡満男）
Tower Building Lobby is 2-stories in height (photo: Mitsuo Matsuoka)

Client: Half Century More Co., Ltd.
Architect for Schematic Design:
    Office of Dennis Cope / Architect and HOK/SF, in association
    (Alex Bonutti, Planning)
    (Alan Bright, Co-designer)
    (Dennis Cope, Programming, Co-designer and Project Manager)
Architect for Design Development: JDC Corporation
Interior Designer for Skilled Nursing/Assisted Living "Plaza Building":
    Graeber, Simmons & Cowan
    (Lea von Kaenel, IIDA and Pollyanna Little, IIDA)

Interior Designer for Independent Living "Tower Building":
    Hirsch-Bedner Associates
    (Michael Sandler)
Landscape Designer: SWA Group/San Francisco
    (John Loomis, designer)
Predominant Contractor: Nippon Kokudo Kaihatsu Co., Ltd.

スカイライトのあるダイニングルームとパティオダイニング（写真：松岡満男）
Dining Room is skylighted and provides patio dining (photo: Mitsuo Matsuoka)

プラザ棟の居住者の目印となる飼鳥籠（写真：小林浩志）
The aviary in the Plaza Building is for all CCRC residents (photo: Koji Kobayashi)

いくつかの注目すべき点。

- 一般的に米国では介護レベルごとに共用部を区画するが、それとは逆にここではさまざまな居住者が2階の共用部を使用することができる。このことでコミュニティの感覚が増強されている。
- 飼鳥籠が2階の目立つ場所にあることで常に自然を感じることができるように配慮されている。
- 同様に、キャンパスの屋内外に豊かに配された緑によって、全ての居住者がいつでも自然を満喫することができる。
- さまざまな広さや種類の共用施設は居住者や家族の交流の場であり、落ち着いた雰囲気の炉辺や楽しいマージャン室、伝統的な茶室、ライブラリー、ダイニング、アルコーブの腰掛け、多目的ルームなどで、居住者の日常に変化と潤いを与えている。

談話エリアと上にメザニンのあるタワー棟のロビー（写真：小林浩志）
Tower Building lobby with seating area and mezzanine overlook (photo: Koji Kobayashi)

サンシティ町田の入口：右にタワー棟（健常棟）と左にプラザ棟（介護棟）（写真：松岡満男）
Sun City Machida entry: Tower Building
(independent living) on the right and Plaza Building (skilled and assisted living) on the left
(photo: Mitsuo Matsuoka)

Several features distinguish this facility:
- Whereas US facilities typically segregate common spaces between the levels of care; the L2 public level of Machida is open, accessible and encouraging to all residents regardless of frailty. This promotes a strong spirit of community.

- The aviary occupies a prominent location and destination on L2, thereby providing a constant contact with Nature.
- Similarly, the numerous indoor and outdoor opportunities given to gardening throughout the campus provide all residents with a perpetual link with the seasons.
- The variety in size, type and focus of common spaces offers the residents and their families with maximum choice for social interaction. Quiet inglenook, active mahjong, traditional tea room, libraries, dining options, seating alcoves and multi-purpose rooms are all available for a diversity in the daily lives of the residents.

タワー棟の2層分のロビーの外観（写真：松岡満男）
Exterior view of Tower Building 2-story lobby (photo: Mitsuo Matsuoka)

全ての方向を見渡せる丘の上のプラザ棟（写真：小林浩志）
Plaza Building - the building sits atop a hill that affords excellent views in all directions (photo: Koji Kobayashi)

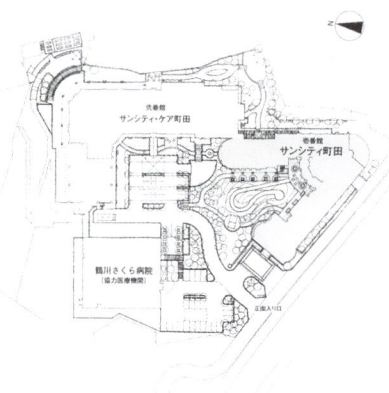

配置図
Site plan

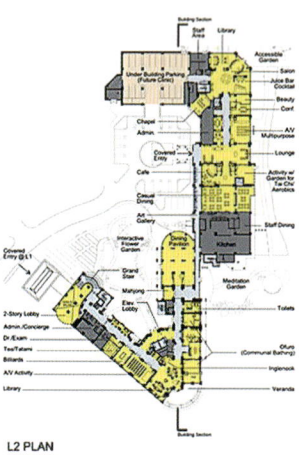

2階全体平面図
Overall floor plan of L2 Public Level

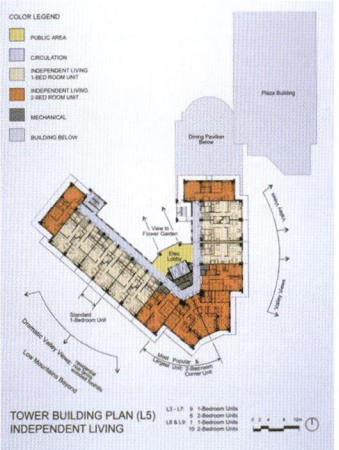

タワー棟の基準階平面図
Tower Building - typical floor plan for independent living residents

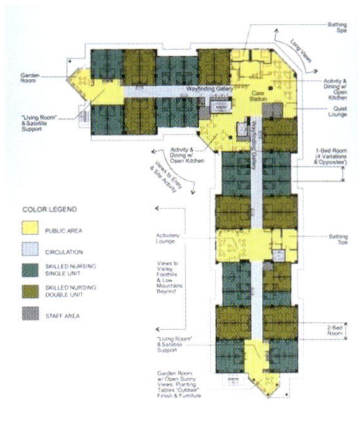

プラザ棟の基準階平面図
Plaza Building - typical floor plan for skilled nursing residents

居室平面図
Unit plan

プラザ棟の居住者のためのガーデンルーム（写真：小林浩志）
A garden room is available on each floor of the Plaza Building for nursing residents (photo: Koji Kobayashi)

Location: Machida-shi, Tokyo Japan
Completion: 2000
Site Area: 14,210 sqm
Gloss Floor Area: 21,280 sqm
    ("Plaza Bldg" = 10,295 sqm; "Tower Bldg" = 10,985 sqm)
Height: "Plaza Bldg" = 5 stories; "Tower Bldg" = 8 stories
Structure: RC and Steel/Concrete structure
Number of Rooms:
    179 nursing and assisted living units
    103 independent living units
Parking: 30 surface spaces; 16 under building spaces
Finishes:
<Predominant Exterior Wall>
    Tile and Glass
<Main lobby>
    Floor: Stone and Carpet
    Wall: Vinyl Wall Covering and Wood
    Ceiling: Gypsum Wallboard
Award: Gold Seal Award - National Council of Seniors' Housing, 2002

タワー棟の音楽室と炉辺（写真：松岡満男）
Tower Building music room with inglenook (photo: Mitsuo Matsuoka)

介護棟の標準ユニット（写真：小林浩志）
Plaza Building - skilled nursing room (photo: Koji Kobayashi)

Sun City Machida
サンシティ町田

都内の希少な森林を望む「皇帝の館」を目指した高齢者居住施設
Independent senior luxury living/CCRC near Tokyo.

右にブリッジを見る玄関前の広場（写真：スティーブ・ホール ©ヘドリッチ・ブレッシング）
Arrival court (photo: Steve Hall © Hedrich Blessing)

215室の健常者用居室などからなるサンシティパーク町田は、東京都の郊外での終身介護施設の第2期施設として建設された。プライバシーが保たれた多くの居室からは、今では貴重な森林の景色を南に望むことができる。
この第2期施設と第1期施設の敷地の間には公道があり、役所の許可を得て2つの敷地を連結するブリッジが架けられた。これによって居住者は双方の施設を安全に行き来しながら、互いの共用施設を使用することができるようになった。

屋根をセットバックさせ平面を雁行させることで、建物のスケールを小気味良く調整することが設計上の戦略であった。建物の構成は、何か皇帝の館を思わせる絵画的なものとなることを目指した。共用部には正面受付やロビーラウンジ、ライブラリー、庭園や森を望むダイニングルームがある。スカイライトのあるプールとスパ棟は伝統的な日本の農家のような形態である。

BAR Architects designed the second phase of this continuing care retirement community, located in the town of Machida near Tokyo. The majority of the 215 independent living units look south into a national forest providing something rare in modern Japan: privacy and forest views for each unit.

The two phases are on opposite sides of a local arterial. The client received permission from the authorities to build a bridge connecting the two phases. This feature allows residents in both phases to share common areas and other areas unique to each phase.

BAR's architectural strategy was to break down the scale of the building vertically by stepping roof heights and horizontally by using an undulating building plan. This type of building massing allowed for a picturesque project-somewhat reminiscent of an emperor's villa. Public spaces include a formal reception, lobby lounge, library, and dining rooms with both garden and forest views. The skylit swimming pool and spa building is shaped like a traditional Japanese farm house.

車寄せの大庇がある玄関ポーチ（写真：スティーブ・ホール © ヘドリッチ・ブレッシング）
Porte cochere (photo: Steve Hall © Hedrich Blessing)

Client: Half Century More Co., Ltd.
Master Designer: BAR Architects
Architect for Schematic Design: BAR Architects
Architect for Design Development: BAR Architects
Interior Designer: Babey Moulton Jue & Booth
Landscape Designer: SWA Group
Predominant Contractor: Shimizu Kensetsu

Location: Machida-shi, Tokyo Japan
Completion: 2003
Site Area: 12,150 sqm
Gross Floor Area: 19,000 sqm
Height: Under ground 1 story; Above ground 9 stories
Structure: Steel and Concrete structure
Number of Rooms: 215 rooms
Parking: 65 cars
Finishes:
<Predominant Exterior Wall>
    Tile and Stone
<Main lobby>
    Floor: Stone
    Wall: Wood and Fabric
    Ceiling: Gypsum Board

ライブラリー（写真：スティーブ・ホール © ヘドリッチ・ブレッシング）
Library (photo: Steve Hall © Hedrich Blessing)

サンシティ町田 025

ダイニングルーム（写真：スティーブ・ホール © ヘドリッチ・ブレッシング）
Dining room (photo: Steve Hall © Hedrich Blessing)

ロビーラウンジ（写真：スティーブ・ホール © ヘドリッチ・ブレッシング）
Lobby lounge (photo: Steve Hall © Hedrich Blessing)

日本建築を想わせるプール棟（写真：スティーブ・ホール © ヘドリッチ・ブレッシング）
Pool building (photo: Steve Hall © Hedrich Blessing)

プライベート・ダイニングルーム
（写真：スティーブ・ホール © ヘドリッチ・ブレッシング）
Private dining room (photo: Steve Hall © Hedrich Blessing)

ピクチャレスクな構図のダイニングルームの夕景（写真：スティーブ・ホール © ヘドリッチ・ブレッシング）
Dining room at night (photo: Steve Hall © Hedrich Blessing)

日本庭園の木立から見るダイニングルーム
（写真：スティーブ・ホール © ヘドリッチ・ブレッシング）
View of dining room from Japanese garden
(photo: Steve Hall © Hedrich Blessing)

プライベート・ダイニングルーム　（写真：スティーブ・ホール © ヘドリッチ・ブレッシング）
Private dining room (photo: Steve Hall © Hedrich Blessing)

サンシティ町田　027

プロムナード（写真：スティーブ・ホール © ヘドリッチ・ブレッシング）
Promenade (photo: Steve Hall © Hedrich Blessing)

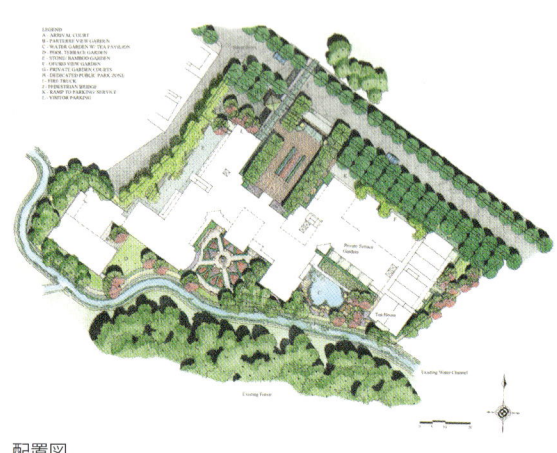

配置図
Site plan

スカイライトのあるプール
（写真：スティーブ・ホール © ヘドリッチ・ブレッシング）
Swimming pool (photo: Steve Hall © Hedrich Blessing)

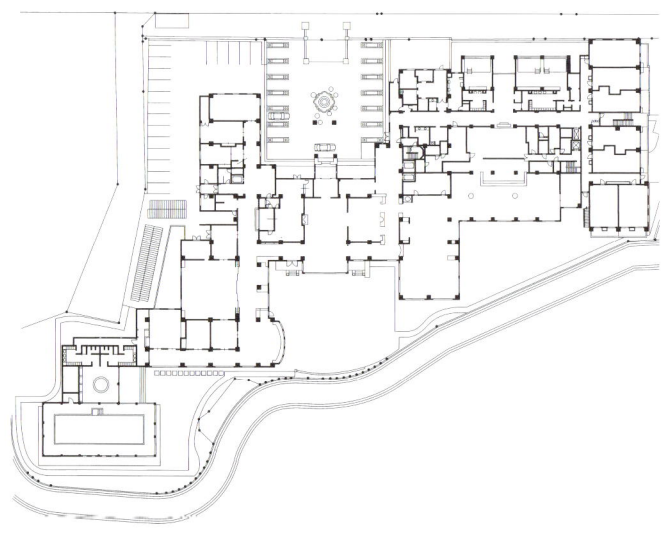

ロビー階平面図
Lobby floor plan

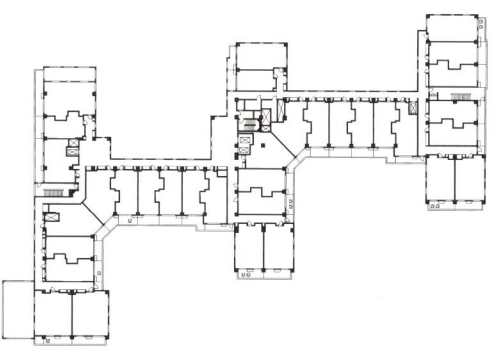

居室階平面図
Residential units floor plan

028　サンシティ町田

ライブラリーの暖炉
(写真：スティーブ・ホール © ヘドリッチ・ブレッシング)
Library fireplace (photo: Steve Hall © Hedrich Blessing)

ロビーの受付
(写真：スティーブ・ホール © ヘドリッチ・ブレッシング)
Lobby reception (photo: Steve Hall © Hedrich Blessing)

ロビーの暖炉 (写真：スティーブ・ホール © ヘドリッチ・ブレッシング)
Lobby fireplace (photo: Steve Hall © Hedrich Blessing)

サンシティ町田　029

Elegano Maya Fosseta Maya

エレガーノ摩耶・フォセッタ摩耶

都心居住の利便性を活かした、自主自立の生活づくり
Place for independency with urbanity at port town.

外観の共通モチーフのグリッドと、曲面状の屋根のスカイラインの隣地公園側外観（写真：古川泰造）
View from an adjacent park looking grid as common motif on facades and skyline with curved surface roof (photo: Taizo Furukawa)

神戸市の中心部に近い東部新都心内のウォーターフロントに建つ、高齢者専用住宅と介護専用型有料老人ホームとの複合施設である。健常入居者が要介護時に移り住みが可能な、終身利用の施設として計画された。

都心居住志向の「アクティブシニア」が活動的で自立した生活を送れるように、ユニバーサルデザインを標榜しながらも、「施設」然としない、快適な「住い＝レジデンス」空間づくりを目指した。

全体構成は、住宅と介護の2つの機能がいずれもスムースに運営されるよう、ゾーンを明快に分割した平面計画とし、動線の交わりを最小限に抑えた。住宅ゾーンでは、車椅子生活と介護のしやすさに配慮した住戸仕様をベースに、メニュープラン方式により多様なライフスタイルに対応。介護ゾーンは中庭中心の回遊型プランとし、明るく開放的な居住空間の提供に努めている。

インテリアは、海外設計事務所と協業しながら、海を間近に望める立地条件を活かした「神戸らしさ」をテーマとする空間演出を行った。ガランと大きな空間になりがちなスケールを細かく分節し、ホテルライクでありながら、住宅的な環境づくりを目指している。

緩やかな曲面の天井と、海に開かれた吹き抜け空間（写真：古川泰造）
Saloon on the 1st floor with gently curved surface ceiling, atrium extending to sea (photo: Taizo Furukawa)

Client: Shinko Care Life Co., Ltd.
Architect for Schematic Design: Takenaka Corporation
Architect for Design Development: Takenaka Corporation
Interior Designer: Babey Moulton Jue & Booth
Predominant Contractor: Takenaka Corporation

The Elegano Maya and Fosseta Maya, located on a waterfront in the east urban core adjacent to center of Kobe, is a complex of senior residences and nursing units. This facility provides residents with continuing care program...resident in the independent room, who needs care is available to move to the care unit.

For the independent "Active Seniors" intending to live within city, design team created not "Institution" but comfortable "Home - residence" with philosophy of universal design.

For effective operations of the two facilities, the building has clear zoning and minimum intersection of circulation of the two facilities. The senior residence is designed to respond variety of lifestyles with basic policy to ease both resident's life with wheelchair and staff's operation for care. Care zone with circulation around a courtyard is spacious and bright with indirect natural light.

Though collaboration with foreign design firm, the design team created spaces respecting characteristics of "Kobe" - a port town. Spacious room is carefully articulated to attain creation of residential environment with elements of hotels.

吹き抜けのサロンに面した、ニッチ的な落ち着いた1階ライブラリー
Comfortable library on the 1st floor off the saloon

土壁と木製ルーバーを使った、陰影のある素材感のクラブハウス外観ディテール（写真：古川泰造）
Detail of clubhouse with quality of mud wall, wood louver, and light and shade (photo: Taizo Furukawa)

多世代コミュニケーションを促す、明るく広いクラブハウスのラウンジ（写真：古川泰造）
Lounge at clubhouse facilitating communication among generations (photo: Taizo Furukawa)

ファミリー向け分譲住宅群と共に一団地を形成することから、シニア世代、ファミリー世代が集えるクラブハウス棟を計画した。開放的で親しみのある表情を創りながら、文化娯楽のための様々な部屋を設ける事で、多世代交流による新しいコミュニティの醸成が期待される。

Within the site housing condominiums along with the facility, a clubhouse provides opportunities both senior generation and family generation to venue. Rooms are prepared to facilitate cultural activities among generations within the community.

大きな開口部と自然素材による開放的で親しみやすいクラブハウス（写真：古川泰造）
Clubhouse with large openings and natural finishes to attain sense of openness and friendly (photo: Taizo Furukawa)

中庭を中心とした、明るい回遊型プランの介護ゾーン（談話コーナー）（写真：古川泰造）
Care zone (seating area) with bright circulation around courtyard (photo: Taizo Furukawa)

グループケア・フロアのダイニング（写真：古川泰造）
Dining at Group care floor (photo: Taizo Furukawa)

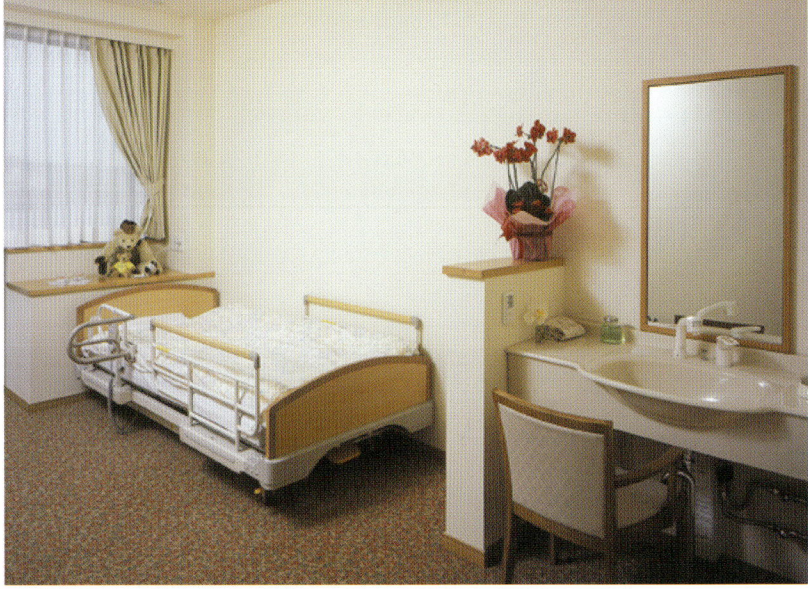

介護居室（写真：古川泰造）
Care unit (photo: Taizo Furukawa)

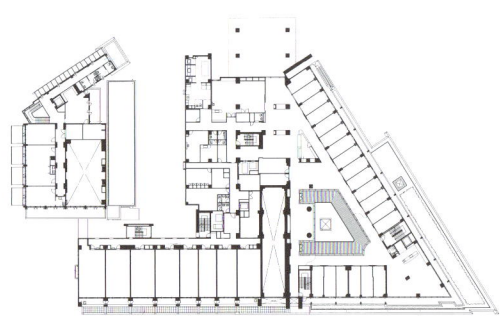

2階平面図
2nd floor plan

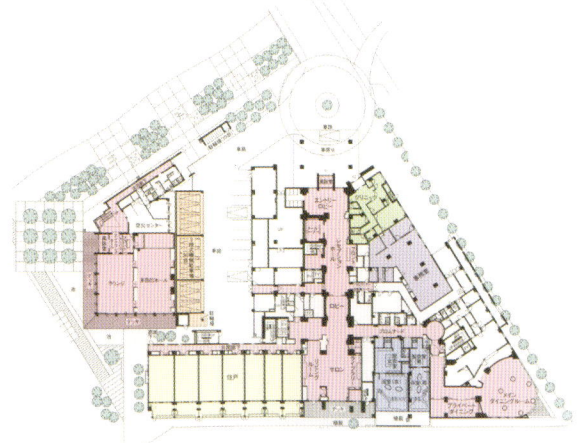

1階平面図
1st floor plan

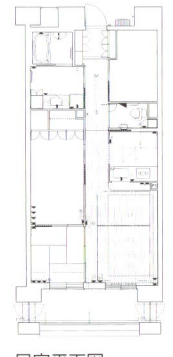

居室平面図
Unit plan

Location: Kobe-shi, Hyogo JAPAN
Completion: 2001
Site Area: 23,354 sqm
Gross Floor Area: (Senior Tower) 21,265 sqm, (Club house) 996 sqm
Height: (Senior Tower) 14 stories; (Club house) 2 stories
Structure: (Senior Tower) SRC+RC, (Club house) RC
Number of Rooms: Senior residence 134, Nursing unit 100
Parking: 36 cars
Finishes:
<Predominant Exterior Wall>
    Mosaic Tile
<Main lobby>
    Floor: Carpet
    Wall: Wall Covering
    Ceiling: Gypsum Board EP

フローリングと白い内装により、船の甲板をイメージした1階メイン・ダイニングルーム（写真：古川泰造）
Main dining room on the 1st floor, use of flooring and white for interior reflects image a deck of ship (photo: Taizo Furukawa)

グリッドモチーフで統一感を与えたファサード（写真：古川泰造）
Grid motif on seaside facade (photo: Taizo Furukawa)

自立生活を支援するため、車椅子生活への対応と介護のしやすさに配慮した。そのため、先行運営されている別施設において、入居者やスタッフへのヒアリング調査及び外部へのアンケート調査を実施。さらにモックアップでのユーザー検証を行う事で、ニーズをきめ細かく分析し、設計に反映させた。

To assist independent life of the residents, design team considered easing both life with wheelchair and caring operation. Prior to design phase, we had found solution of those through interviews and questionnaires with residents and staff at other preceding facilities. Also the design carefully reflected result of analysis learned from needs of user through mockup.

健常入居者用住戸（リビング）（写真：古川泰造）
Residence in Independent living area (living room) (photo: Taizo Furukawa)

River Landing at Sandy Ridge
リバーランディング・サンディリッジ

ゴルフコースに展開するリタイアメントコミュニティ
Replacement retirement community developed on an existing 127-acre golf course site.

上空から見た本館（写真：ジェリー・デイビス、アエリアル・エイズ・インク）
Aerial view of the facility's primary building (photo: Jerry Davis, Aerial Ads, Inc.)

美しいゴルフコースを持つこの高齢者コミュニティは、継続的なケアを必要とする居住者のために82億円をかけてつくられた。この魅力的なコミュニティを創出するために既存の湖や木立が保全されている。約510,000平方メートルの既存の9ホールのゴルフ場がオープンスペースとして、クラスター棟やコミュニティ棟およびヴィレッジの中心部を視覚的に結び付けている。
コテージは居住者同士が親近感を得られるようにグルーピングされている他、コミュニティ活動のさまざまなアメニティにも接しやすくなっている。

建物の周囲では釣りや園芸、クロケット、ゴルフなどの野外活動を楽しむことができる。居間には外からの光が射し込み、そこにいれば自然の景色が目に映り、居住者は外の庭や洒落たポーチ、パティオでの時間を楽しむことができる。居住者やビジターはプライベートポーチやバルコニーからゴルフコースや自然環境などの様子を見ることができる。また工夫を凝らした創りの共用部のポーチやパティオが、屋内と屋外でのアクティビティが接する付近に設置されている。

This $59 million replacement retirement community is designed to engage all residents throughout the continuum of care with the beautiful golf course setting. In developing this active adult community, designers retained lakes, woodlots and nine holes of the existing 127-acre golf course site as open spaces that visually link neighborhood groupings to the community building and village core.

Cottages residences are grouped in smaller, intimate groupings that cluster residents and position neighborhood groupings near and accessible to a concentration of amenities that focus the community activity.

Throughout the community, exterior rooms created by building configuration, are activated by the availability of outdoor activities such as fishing, tennis, putting greens, croquet and golf. Living spaces are designed to bring the natural environment inside through light and view and to invite residents to enjoy the pleasantly detailed and comfortably scaled outdoor courtyards, porches and patios. Private porches and balconies provide residents and visitors with views to the golf course, natural surroundings, and areas of outdoor activity while public porches and patios with varying degrees of enclosure and shade are located near concentrated areas of indoor and outdoor activity.

Client: The Presbyterian Homes, Inc.
Master Designer: FreemanWhite, Inc.
Architect for Schematic Design: FreemanWhite, Inc.
Architect for Design Development: FreemanWhite, Inc.
Interior Designer: Design Associates, Inc.
Landscape Designer: J.R. McAdams Company, Inc.
Predominant Contractor: Bovis Lend Lease

共用部の居間（写真：ティム・ブックマン）
Common area - living room (photo: Tim Buchman)

メイン・ダイニングルーム（写真：ティム・ブックマン）
Formal dining room (photo: Tim Buchman)

居室のダイニングとキッチン（写真：ビリー・シムコックス、フリーマンホワイト・インク）
Dining/kitchen area in private residence (photo: Billy Simcox, FreemanWhite, Inc.)

クラブルーム。郵便受けとガラス戸越しにビリヤード場を見る（写真：ティム・ブックマン）
Club room and mailing-billiard window (photo: Tim Buchman)

共用部の居間の屋内バルコニー（写真：ティム・ブックマン）
Interior balcony at commons living room (photo: Tim Buchman)

居室の居間（写真：ビリー・シムコックス、フリーマンホワイト・インク）
Living room in private residence (photo: Billy Simcox, FreemanWhite, Inc.)

施設の雰囲気を保つために、サービス部門の動線は居住者のものと交差しないように配慮されている。さらに、ウェルネスプログラムへの専用のアクセスを設けることで、居住者の健康管理の促進とアパートメントやコテージの独立性が保たれている。

To protect the facility's ambiance, service areas are discreetly located to facilitate the delivery of materials and services without crossing paths of resident travel. Additionally, separate access to the wellness programs from different areas of the community prevents residents from healthcare or the apartments and cottages from crossing paths.

居室の寝室（写真：ビリー・シムコックス、フリーマンホワイト・インク）
Bedroom in private residence (photo: Billy Simcox, FreemanWhite, Inc.)

River Landing at Sandy Ridge

介護ユニットのダイニングエリア（写真：ティム・ブックマン）
Dining area in skilled nursing unit (photo: Tim Buchman)

メモリーサポート・ユニットの居間（写真：ティム・ブックマン）
Living room in memory support unit (photo: Tim Buchman)

9番ホールから見た居住棟の外観（写真：ティム・ブックマン）
Exterior view from ninth hole, features resident (photo: Tim Buchman)

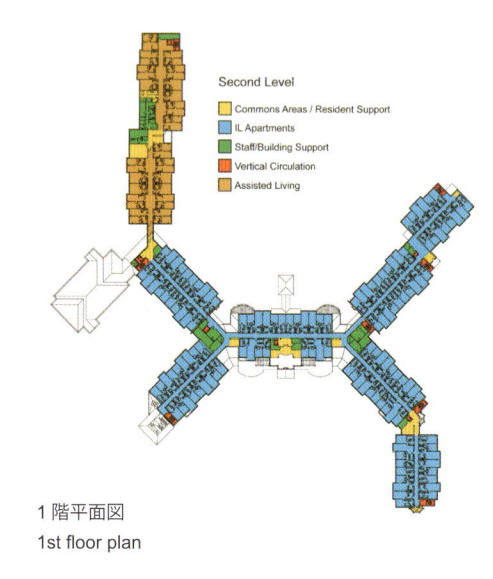

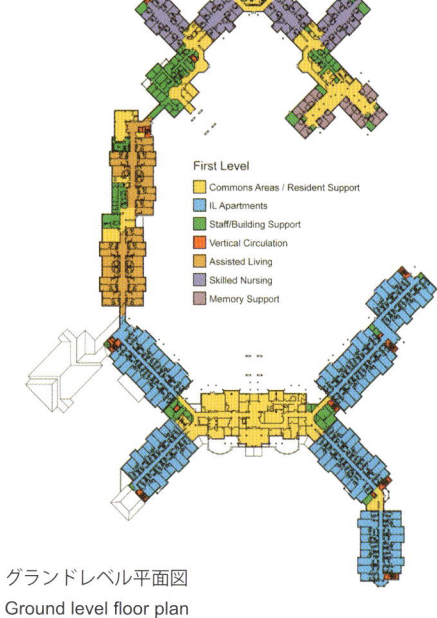

1階平面図
1st floor plan

居室平面図
Unit plan

グランドレベル平面図
Ground level floor plan

Location: Colfax, North Carolina U.S.A.
Completion: 2003
Renovation/Extension: 2003
Site Area: 242,800 sqm, 513,900 sqm
Gross Floor Area: 49,850 sqm
Height: Ground level plus 3 above ground stories
Structure:
    Structural steel with composite steel and concrete floor slab
    Wood roof trusses except at Healthcare which has steel trusses
Number of Rooms:
    142 apartments
    85 cottages
    43 skilled nursing beds
    40 assisted living units
    16 dementia units
Parking: 425 cars in open surface lots
Finishes:
<Predominant Exterior Wall>
    Brick with Composite Shingle Roof
<Main lobby>
    Floor: Carpet
    Wall: Vinyl Wall
    Ceiling: GWB / Acoustical
Award and year: Design 2002: Nursing Homes (LTCM), Project in Progress

テラスから見た外観（写真：ティム・ブックマン）
Exterior view from terrace (photo: Tim Buchman)

ウェルネスセンターのプール（写真：ティム・ブックマン）
Pool in wellness center (photo: Tim Buchman)

上空から見た施設と敷地（写真：ジェリー・デイビス、アエリアル・エイズ・インク）
Aerial of the facility and site (photo: Jerry Davis, Aerial Ads, Inc.)

River Landing at Sandy Ridge 041

Grünes Heim Shinyamanote
グリューネスハイム新山手

総合病院・介護老人保健施設と連携する豊かな暮らしの場
A medical mansion supported by cooperative service of hospital and healthcare facility.

斜面上にテラスがある食堂（写真：フォトワークス）
Dining with terrace on the hill (photo: PHOTO-WORKS)

既存の病院と介護老人保健施設に隣接する立地を活かし、健康に不安のある高齢者を主な対象とした自立生活型の賃貸メディカルマンションである。
敷地は緑豊かな丘陵の麓の傾斜地にあり、敷地内にはイチョウなどの既存樹木を多く残している。敷地内の中庭や遊歩道をはじめ、建物の様々な場所からこれらの自然や四季の移り変わりを楽しめるようにしている。
共用部にはラウンジや食堂、テラスだけでなくバルコニーのある廊下も用意されている。建物全体を生活空間と捉えた場づくりを建物内外に展開することにより、「お気に入りの場所」や「いつものところ」を住み手が見つけ、そこに出会いや集いが生まれることを意図している。
一方、住戸は南向きとした他、奥行きのあるバルコニーと一体的に利用できるワイドリビングを中心とした間取りにより、日常生活を一番快適な場所で過ごせるようにしている。
こうした場づくりとともに、熟練したスタッフによる施設運営が住まい手の安心できる豊かな生活を支えている。

Client: Japan Anti-Tuberculosis Association
Architect for Schematic Design: Kajima Design
Architect for Design Development: Kajima Design
Predominant Contractor: Kajima Corporation

東側から見る住戸棟と食堂（写真：フォトワークス）
View of resident building and dining from east (photo: PHOTO-WORKS)

The Grunes Heim Shinyamanote, adjacent to existing hospital and health care facility, is a lease-medical-mansion for the independent living elderly who are frail in their healthy.

The site on a slope at foot of greenery-hill has a lot of existing maidenhair trees and others. Through courtyards and pathways in the site, residents enjoy to see nature, and feel change of season.

Lounge, terrace and corridor with balcony are in common area. Spaces distributed inside as well as outside of the facility conclude life of the residents, and give them opportunities to find places for their "comfort" and "preference" along with facilitating encounters or venues with others.

Unit with wide living room extending to deep balcony faces south, and is the most comfortable place for their life.

Development of these places and operation by experienced staff support safety in life of the residents.

十分な奥行きと広さのある正面玄関（写真：フォトワークス）
Main entry with spacious poach (photo: PHOTO-WORKS)

意図的な段差のある食堂（写真：フォトワークス）
Dining area with steps stimulating residents (photo: PHOTO-WORKS)

住戸は1人または2人の世帯を想定しワンルームまたは1LDKの間取りを用意し、引戸の採用により車椅子の利用を見据えたゆとりある空間を作り出している。また居室には収納を設けず、慣れ親しんだ家具に囲まれた部屋作りができるようにしている。

One bedrooms and two bedrooms prepared for singles or couples are spacious and apply sliding door for wheelchair use. To facilitate creation of environment surrounded by preferable furniture, there isn't any storage in the room.

住棟と職員住戸の間の中庭（写真：フォトワークス）
Courtyard between resident building and staff building (photo: PHOTO-WORKS)

引戸によって自由度の高い居室（写真：フォトワークス）
Resident room using sliding doors to attain flexibility (photo: PHOTO-WORKS)

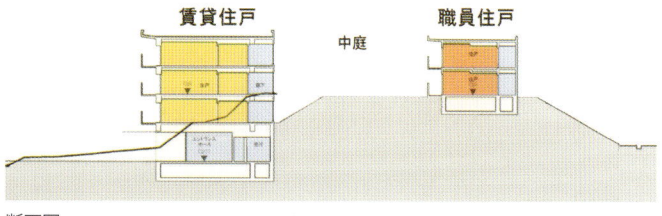

断面図
Section

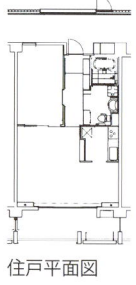

住戸平面図
Unit plan

Location: Higashimurayama-shi, Tokyo Japan
Completion: 2004
Site Area: 4,828 sqm
Gross Floor Area: 4,061 sqm
Height: Under ground 1 story; Above ground 4 stories
Structure: Concrete structure
Number of Rooms: 37 rooms
Parking: 10 cars
Finishes:
<Predominant Exterior Wall>
　Ceramic Tile
<Main lobby>
　Floor: Flooring
　Wall: EP
　Ceiling: EP

グリューネスハイム新山手

メインアプローチ（写真：フォトワークス）
Main approach (photo: PHOTO-WORKS)

配置図
Site plan

同一経営による総合病院と介護老人保健施設との連携により、24時間体制での緊急時対応を可能としている。一方日常的には専門家による生活指導や健康相談など、自立しながらも高齢者の不安を取り除き安心して暮らせる場を提供している。

24 hours operation including for emergency is served through cooperation of a healthcare facility with a general hospital - both are managed by same body. Usually, experts provide the resident with life guidance and health counseling to remove their anxious and support their life.

中庭を照らす共用部の階段（写真：フォトワークス）
Staircase lighting courtyard in the evening (photo: PHOTO-WORKS)

グリューネスハイム新山手

Peninsula Regent

ペニンシュラ・リージェント

フルレンジのホテルサービス付の豪華な高齢者高層居住施設
High-rise independent living and personal care units incorporating a full range of hotel services.

エル・カミノ・レアル通りから見た外観（写真：ドゥグ・ダン、BAR アーキテクツ）
View from El Camino Real (photo: Doug Dun / BAR Architects)

ペニンシュラ・リージェントは、207室の健常者用ユニットと20室のパーソナルケア・スイーツからなる10階建ての高齢者用の豪華な居住施設である。サンメトロのダウンタウンに位置するこのプロジェクトでは、200席のクラブ・レストランや共用諸室、健康維持施設、屋内プールなどが設置されている他、居住者はあらゆる種類のホテルサービスを受けることができる。ペニンシュラ・リージェントは、この地域では初の高層の高級高齢者居住施設であったため、その設計を巡ってコミュニティの理解を得ることが重要であった。

The Peninsula Regent is a 10-story luxury housing development for seniors consisting of 207 independent living units and 20 personal care suites. Situated in downtown San Mateo, California, the project incorporates a full range of hotel services for the occupants, including a 200-seat club/restaurant, public rooms, exercise rooms, and a covered swimming pool. The Peninsula Regent was one of the first high-rise luxury senior housing facilities on the peninsula and therefore community support was important to the design process.

緑に囲まれたダイニングルームのテラス（写真：ドゥグ・ダン、BAR アーキテクツ）
Dining room terrace (photo: Doug Dun / BAR Architects)

Client: BAC Associates
Master Designer: BAR Architects
Architect for Schematic Design: BAR Architects
Architect for Design Development: BAR Architects
Landscape Designer: Emery Rogers
Predominant Contractor: Stolte

ワンベッドルームの入口付近から見る居間（写真：デニス・アンダーソン）
One-Bedroom residential unit entry (photo: Dennis Anderson)

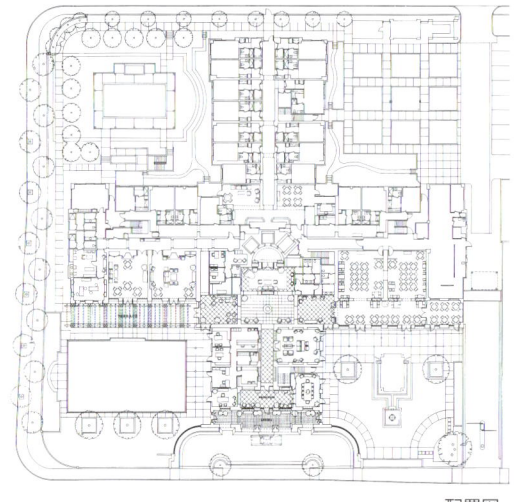

配置図
Site plan

南西の眺め（写真：ドゥグ・ダン / BAR アーキテクツ）
Southwest view (photo: Doug Dun / BAR Architects)

Location: San Mateo, CA U.S.A.
Completion: 1988
Site Area: 8,900 sqm
Gross Floor Area: 27,870 sqm
Height: 10 stories
Structure: Concrete structure
Number of Rooms: 207 rooms
Parking: 272 cars
Finishes:
<Predominant Exterior Wall>
    Cement Plaster
<Main lobby>
    Floor: Stone and Carpet
    Wall: Plaster
    Ceiling: Plaster and Wood Trim
Award: Grand Award, Gold Nugget, 1990; Gold Seal Award, NAHB/NCSH, 1992

ワンベッドルーム（写真：デニス・アンダーソン）
One-bedroom unit (photo: Dennis Anderson)

居室平面図
Unit plan

ツーベッドルーム（写真：デニス・アンダーソン）
Two-bedroom unit (photo: Dennis Anderson)

Peninsula Regent 049

Will Mark Kashiihama
ウィルマーク香椎浜

新興都市での利便性に恵まれた先進的なシニアマンション
Senior maison providing advanced program in a new town.

せっ器質タイル等で仕上げた、シックなデザインの外観（写真：濱田一郎）
Gently designed facade finished by ceramic tile (photo: Ichiro Hamada)

九州一の繁華街である福岡市天神から、都市高速経由バスで19分、すぐ隣には大型ショッピングセンター・イオン香椎浜SCがあるウィルマーク香椎浜は、キャナルシティ博多等の都市開発、またグランドハイアット福岡などのホテル事業を経営する福岡地所グループによって設立された介護付有料老人ホームである。

11階建ての健常棟は全戸南向きで、大理石貼りのエントランスロビーを通り抜けると、ビリヤードコーナーやライブラリーを備える豪華なラウンジがあり、ホテルを髣髴させる。その他、市街を一望できる展望浴場、フィットネスルーム、AVルーム、カルチャールーム、理美容室などの共用施設が充実している。また、全戸2面採光の角部屋を実現した介護棟は3階建てで、自然光の入る中庭を取り囲むように配置され、非常に明るく広い住空間が整っている。そこでは24時間体制の看護とクリニックの嘱託医との連携による万全の看護・介護体制でハイレベルな運営が行われている。

The Will Mark Kashiihama for continuum of elderly care, adjacent to a shopping center - AEON Kashiihama - is on a site with 19 minutes express bus ride from the busiest place in Kusyu -Fukuoka Tenjin. Developer - the Fukuoka Jisho Group- operates the Canal City Hakata and the Ground Hyatt Fukuoka.

Entrance lobby finished by marble stone like that of in hotels, billiard area, library, and lounge are on the first floor in the eleven stories independent building accommodating all units facing to south. Other common area includes communal bath with panoramic view, fitness room, AV room, cultural room, and beauty saloon. Common area of the three stories of care building is lit by natural light through courtyard, and all of corner units are bright enough by double sided natural light. High-level operation combines 24 hours care system with medical service by commissioned doctor.

一流ホテルのような気品と安らぎで迎える500角の大理石貼りのエントランスロビー（写真：濱田一郎）
Noble and comfortable entrance lobby like hotels, finished by 500 x 500 marble stones (photo: Ichiro Hamada)

洗練されたインテリアに囲まれ、気ままなひと時を過ごせるクラブラウンジ（写真：濱田一郎）
Club lounge with sophisticated environment for casual use (photo: Ichiro Hamada)

マスタープラン
Master plan

Client: Fukuoka Jisho Seniorlife Co., Ltd.
Architect for Schematic Design: Kumesekkei Co., Ltd.
Architect for Design Development: Kumesekkei Co., Ltd.
Interior Designer: ILYA Co., Ltd.
Landscape Designer: Kumesekkei Co., Ltd.
Collaborator: Design Network Co., Ltd
Predominant Contractor: Taisei Corporation

建物の内外に渡り共用空間の充実を図っている。特に介護棟は明るい平面計画となるよう、3つの中庭を中心に居室やリビングダイニングを配しており、施設内に居ても時間の変化や四季の変化を感じることができる計画となっている。

Three courtyards at the care building have particular bright units and common living/dining areas and provide residents with sense of season.

大画面のTV、マッサージ機も装備したリラクゼーションラウンジ（写真：濱田一郎）
Relaxation lounge with large TV screen and massage machine (photo: Ichiro Hamada)

光や風、季節や時間の変化を感じる介護棟の光庭（写真：濱田一郎）
Courtyard of care facility with sense of season and time of a day
(photo: Ichiro Hamada)

窓越しに市街を見晴らせるスカイスパ（写真：濱田一郎）
Sky spa overlooking city though large window
(photo: Ichiro Hamada)

庭園を望む介護棟専用のスライドインバス（写真：濱田一郎）
Slide-in bath of care facility views garden
(photo: Ichiro Hamada)

ワイドな窓越しに広がる庭園を眺めるダイニングレストラン（春夏秋冬）（写真：濱田一郎）
Dining with view to garden though large window (Four Season) (photo: Ichiro Hamada)

壁面全体に書棚を設けたライブラリー（写真：濱田一郎）
Library with built-in selves (photo: Ichiro Hamada)

本施設の設計に際し、ホテル事業で培ったホスピタリティのノウハウと、福岡地所が母体となって設立した社会福祉法人が運営する高齢者福祉施設で培った介護のノウハウを結集して、従来の高齢者施設とは違う、住環境のより優れた設計を行った。

Design team focused on creation of an unique and comfortable facility beyond any other forerunners, by fusing hospitality of hotels and services of care centers, which we learned though our relative business on these fields.

プライベート・ダイニング（写真：濱田一郎）
Private dining room (photo: Ichiro Hamada)

ウィルマーク香椎浜 053

全戸南向きで、半数以上が2面採光と通風をかなえた健常棟角住戸（写真：濱田一郎）
Residents room, facing south, has double sided natural light and ventilation (photo: Ichiro Hamada)

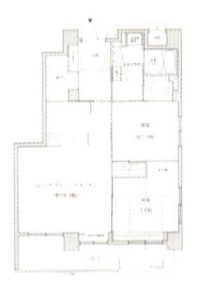

居室平面図
Unit plan

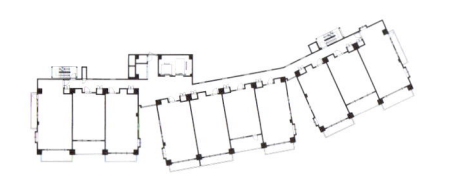

住戸階平面図
Residents room floor plan

配置図/1階平面図
Site plan/1st floor plan

Location: Fukuoka-shi, Fukuoka Japan
Completion: 2005
Site Area: 7,298 sqm
Gross Floor Area: 14,351 sqm
Height: 11 stories
Structure: Reinforced Concrete structure
Number of Rooms: 159 rooms
Parking: 34 cars
Finishes:
<Predominant Exterior Wall>
　　　Ceramic Tile
<Main lobby>
　　　Floor: Marble Stone
　　　Wall: Marble Stone with Wood and Paint
　　　Ceiling: Paint

2面採光と通風をかなえた24平方メートルの介護棟角住戸（写真：濱田一郎）
24 sqm of corner care unit with double sided natural light and ventilation
(photo: Ichiro Hamada)

楽しいシニアリビングのために
　-スローライフの家づくり、世代間交流を進める街づくり

段差がないことだけがバリアフリーではありません。バリアフリーのためには利用を阻害するあらゆる要因を取り除く必要があります。和室の床から立ち上がることも、廊下を介して遠くにあるトイレにいくことも、年とともに億劫になりがちです。上下の移動もさることながら、「遠い」ということもバリアーとなります。トイレが遠い、玄関が遠いこともバリアーとなっています。居室に隣接するトイレ、居室の縁側越しに見られる庭やすぐに出られる通り・路地であれば気軽にスローライフを楽しむことができるのではないでしょうか。少子高齢化の進む中、高齢者の為というのではなく、スローライフを楽しめる住環境づくりは一般化しつつある重要なテーマです。壮年夫婦に子供という核家族を想定して作られたｎＬＤＫの住宅とは違う形が今の住まいに求められています。

1. すべての部屋はリビングのように
住宅ではすべての部屋はリビングのように、生活を楽しむ場であることが必要です。廊下も移動のためだけの機能を持つ空間ではなく、歩くことを楽しむリビングであり、浴室前の脱衣所も湯上がりのくつろぎを楽しめる身近なリビング空間となります。玄関や共用廊下も隣人と顔を会わせられる交流空間です。もっともっと楽しい廊下に、楽しい玄関にしていく必要があります。

2. 機能はコンパクトに
住宅で求められる機能はそれほどパーフェクトである必要はありません。コンビニのように手軽に身近に必要なものがそろうことが重要です。身近にすべての機能がコンパクトに満足されることが求められます。機能分化ではなく混在であり、何が必要か、兼用してもよいのは何かを見極めながら、手の届くところにコンパクトに揃えるのがポイントです。

3. 空間はオープンに
プライバシーを優先してつくられた間仕切壁や廊下は、家族の変化とともに障害となることがあります。家族が少人数にかわり、高齢化していくと、身近にリビング、身近にトイレ・浴室があることの方が手軽で楽しい生活空間となります。さらに、サポートを必要と

共用部のイメージスケッチ
Sketch for common area

リビングの感覚の共用部のイメージスケッチ
Sketch for common area with sense of a living room

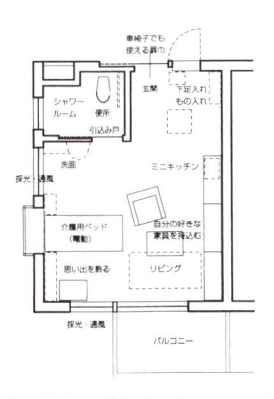

必要なものが身近にあるユニットの概念
Everything close to residents in a unit

For Enjoyable Senior Living
　- Creation of a house for slow life with socialization among multiple generations

Barrier free is not attained solely by elimination of differences between floors but complemented by removing all factors to obstruct use of place. For the elderly distance besides vertical movement becomes barrier, too. Such barrier includes lavatory, entry and other function at distant location as well as tatami floor. The enjoyable slow life easily could be attained through a lavatory adjacent to a resident room, garden visible from a window of the room, or a street/passage directly accessible from the room. In tendency of declining birthrate and a growing proportion of elderly people, creation of living environment for the enjoyable slow life has become a prevailing theme. Substitution of conventional nLDK (a typical unit style with Private rooms, a Living room, a Dining room and a Kitchen for model family of a couple and children) is needed for a house of today.

1. Sense of a living room for the all other rooms
A house should be filled with places to enjoy life. A corridor could be a living room to enjoy walking; a change area could be so to enjoy relaxing after bathing; and common areas could be place for socialization. Far more enjoyable corridor and entry should be prepared.

2. Compact function
Compactly prepared function close to them is needed. Rather than separation of function, compact and mixed arrangement of them from viewpoints of needs and multiple services is key for creation of successful places.

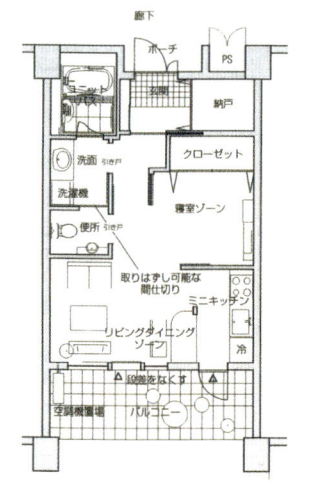

必要なものが身近にある住戸の概念
Everything close to residents in a room

趣味の物が近くにある生活空間のイメージスケッチ
Sketch for living environment with resident's interest

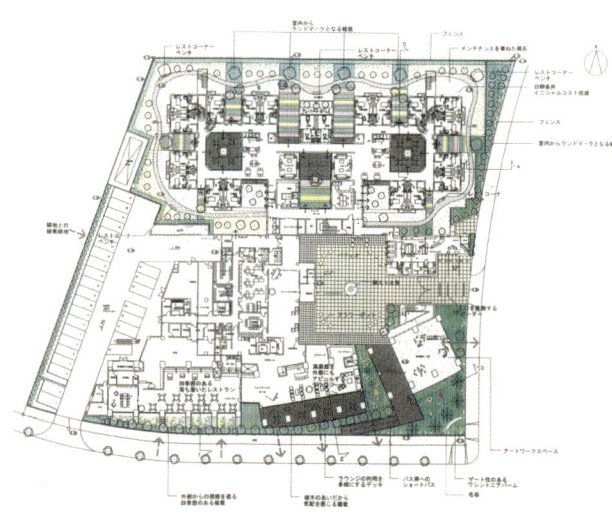

屋内のどこに居ても屋外を感じられる施設
Facility with sense of out side all around

するお年寄りにはサポートを受け入れやすい出入り口やスペースの余裕が不可欠となります。廊下をなくし、間仕切りには予備のヘルプドア、玄関には広いドアを設けるなど、使いこなす家でなく居ながら使えるフレキシブルなつくりが求められてきます。

4. 仕上げはカスタマイズ

高齢者にとってライフスタイルを変えることはとても難しい作業です。住み慣れた家・街で一生を全うしたいものです。そのためには家や住む場所が変わったとしても、マイスタイル、マイペースを貫ける住環境づくりが肝要です。ノスタルジックに昔と全く同じ我が家を実現することはありませんが、好みやわがままを通し、自分らしさを表現できるところが必要です。内装仕上げやしつらえにはマイスペースを表現する場が欠かせません。更には照明や空調なども個別コントロールで個人の好みに合わせる工夫が必要となるでしょう。

5. 変化のあるリズム

どんなにすばらしい環境も、生活も動きの少ないお年寄りにとってマンネリに陥りがちです。四季の変化や趣味サークルの人付き合いなど、程よい刺激に誘われてアクティブに活動する場面も必要です。屋外環境や街角の風景を取り込み家の外と交わる演出ももとめられます。
引きこもりにならないためにも、家の外の自然や、近所付き合いを大切に、それらを誘う家づくり・施設づくりが望まれます。

都心では小学校が減り、高齢者向けの施設にかわる光景をよく目にします。少子高齢化のなか地域社会の状況が変わりそれに対応したかに見えます。しかし相変わらず機能分化された施設が多く、地域社会に馴染めない例も多いのが実情です。保育所と高齢者福祉施設の合築や医療施設を併設した高齢者住宅づくりなど、お年寄りと子供たちの世代間交流を積極的に誘う機能融合する施設づくりが進み、これからの活性ある地域社会の街づくりに貢献することが期待されています。

株式会社久米設計
児玉耕二

3. Open spaces

For a smaller family of the elderly, close location of living room, lavatory and bathroom could facilitate enjoyable life in the house. To attain a house with flexibility for easy use, large enough doorway and place to accept assist for their life are essential.

4. Customized finishes

To correspond to their wants to age at the same place, providing sense of my style and my space even in new facility or place is essential. Opportunity for presenting their identity could be prepared through finishes and furniture in the place, along with individually controllable light and air-conditioning for the environment.

5. Rhythm with diversity

Even in a charming environment, life of the elderly with less activity tends to fall into isolated mannerism. A house with natural environment, communication with neighborhood through activity could resolve the situation.

Recently in urban area, renovations of elementary school to facility of the elderly are easily seen. But they are individually allocated function among the urban fabric. Facility with mixed function for children, the elderly with health care should contribute to creation of town with sense of vitality.

Koji Kodama, Architect (JIA)
Kumesekkei Co., Ltd.

第二章
既存施設の機能を高レベルで強化した
リノベーション型

Chapter Two
Strategic Repositioning

Bridgepoint Assisted Living
ブリッジポイント・アシステッドリビング

サンフランシスコの歴史的建築物の魅力と快適さを併せ持つキャンパス
Assisted Senior Living Facility combines the attraction of San Francisco historic architecture with modern amenities.

既存の樹木と歴史的建築物を活かした正面外観（写真：ドゥグ・ダン、BAR アーキテクツ）
Front elevation historic building (photo: Doug Dun / BAR Architects)

ブリッジポイント介護付高齢者居住施設は、サンフランシスコの歴史的建築物の魅力と現代的な快適さを併せ持つ雰囲気のキャンパスである。計画範囲には、ランドマークであるシュリナーズ小児病院の再生と、その後背地での増築を含んでいる。この計画では敷地の歴史的特徴や既存の芝生、樹木を保全しながら、施設に明るい中庭を創出することを意図している。
ブリッジポイントにはスタジオタイプからツーベッドルームに至るまで120室のさまざまな種類の居室がある。広々とした共用部にはダイニングルームやウェルネスセンター、ライブラリー、テクノロジーセンター、理美容室、音楽室などがある。壁画やモザイク模様のタイル、什器、扉などの歴史的要素によって、この建物の創設された往時を想い起こすことができる。
敷地の手入れや玄関の再生、新しい中庭の設置、共用部の用途転換などによる活性化、調和する様式を用いた増築など、ここではさまざまな工夫が施されている。

既存建物と新築建物とに囲まれた南側の中庭（写真：ドゥグ・ダン、BAR アーキテクツ）
South courtyard (photo: Doug Dun / BAR Architects)

The Bridgepoint Assisted Senior Living Facility combines the attraction of San Francisco historic architecture with modern amenities in a campus atmosphere. Featuring the rehabilitated landmark Shriners Hospital for Children, the campus includes the addition of a modern building to the rear that more than doubles the project area. The addition dovetails with the historic building to create sunny courtyards, while maintaining the historic characteristics of the property, the open lawn and trees.

With a wide variety in its 120 dwelling units, Bridgepoint offers a choice of unit sizes ranging from studios to two-bedroom apartments. Extensive common areas are located throughout the complex, including a dining room, wellness center, library, technology center, beauty salon, and music room.

Client: Bridgepoint Assisted Living
Master Designer: BAR Architects
Architect for Schematic Design: BAR Architects
Architect for Design Development: BAR Architects
Interior Designer: Disrud & Associates (Carol Disrud)
Landscape Designer: The Office of Cheryl Barton
Predominant Contractor: Cahill Contractors

Restored historic elements such as a painted mural, tile mosaics, fixtures and doors remind residents of the previous era of the building.

Principal features of the building include: the restored entry; the creation of new courtyards; the rehabilitation of the estate grounds; the revitalization of commons spaces for new uses; and stylistically compatible new addition.

この場をランドマークとすることでこの貴重な歴史的建築物と敷地を保全しようと、コミュニティは計画に積極的な係わりを示した。近隣への配慮から、最終的なデザインは元の小児病院の邸宅のような特徴を活かしたものとなった。

The community stepped forward to save this beloved historic structure and grounds by landmarking the site. By responding to the neighborhood sentiment, the final design successfully recaptured the estate-like qualities of the original children's hospital.

日当たりのよい開放的なティーテラス（写真：ドゥグ・ダン、BAR アーキテクツ）
Tea terrace (photo: Doug Dun / BAR Architects)

歴史的建築物を活かした正面外観（写真：ドゥグ・ダン、BAR アーキテクツ）
Front elevation historic building (photo: Doug Dun / BAR Architects)

歴史的建築物を活かした表玄関（写真：ドゥグ・ダン、BAR アーキテクツ）
Main entry historic building (photo: Doug Dun / BAR Architects)

共用部のライブラリーとグランドピアノが置かれた前室（写真：ドゥグ・ダン、BAR アーキテクツ）
Common library (photo: Doug Dun / BAR Architects)

受付とロビー（写真：ドゥグ・ダン、BAR アーキテクツ）
Reception and Lobby area (photo: Doug Dun / BAR Architects)

バルコニーのある共用部のダイニングルーム（写真：ドゥグ・ダン、BAR アーキテクツ）
Common dining room (photo: Doug Dun / BAR Architects)

Bridgepoint Assisted Living 061

天井の高い壁画のあるファインアートルーム（写真：ドゥグ・ダン、BAR アーキテクツ）
Fine arts room (photo: Doug Dun / BAR Architects)

配置図
Site plan

歴史的建築物の背後に 4 階建の介護付複合施設を創ることによって十分な大きさのものが確保できた。この増築はプロジェクトの全体面積の 8,740 平方メートルの約 2/3 に相当し、歴史的特徴を保ちながら街の中心部にキャンパスのような環境を創出するものである。

Creating a large enough building to accommodate an assisted living complex was solved with the introduction of a 4-story addition located entirely within the "view shadow" behind the historic building. This addition accommodates nearly two-thirds of the project's 94,000 square feet, retains the project's historic character and creates a sheltered campus-like environment in the heart of the city.

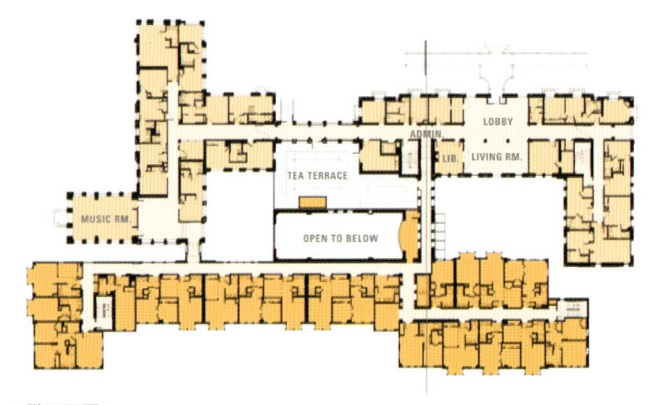

2 階平面図
2nd floor plan

居室平面図
Unit plan

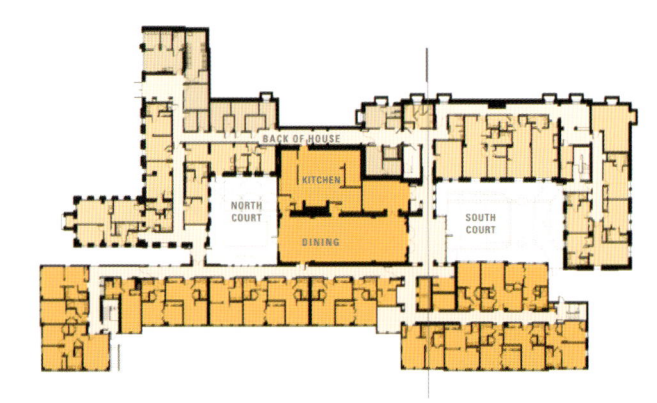

1 階平面図
1st floor plan

Location: San Francisco, CA U.S.A.
Completion: 2001
Renovation/Extension: 5,290 sqm (new)/3,440 sqm (remodel)
Site Area: 9,230 sqm
Gross Floor Area: 8,730 sqm
Height:
    (1/remodel) under ground and 4/
    addition (2/remodel) above ground stories
Structure: Concrete structure
Number of Rooms: 120 rooms
Parking: 12 cars
Finishes:
<Predominant Exterior Wall>
    Cement Plaster
<Main lobby>
    Floor: Carpet
    Wall: Gypsum Board with Wood Trim
    Ceiling: Gypsum Board with Wood Trim
    Award: San Francisco Beautiful Award, 2001

暖炉のあるカジュアルな雰囲気のエンリッチメント・センター
（写真：ドゥグ・ダン、BAR アーキテクツ）
Enrichment center (photo: Doug Dun / BAR Architects)

北側を見る建物の外観（写真：ドゥグ・ダン、BAR アーキテクツ）
Front elevation looking north (photo: Doug Dun / BAR Architects)

歴史的建築物を活かした居室（写真：ドゥグ・ダン、BAR アーキテクツ）
Historic building unit bedroom (photo: Doug Dun / BAR Architects)

Bridgepoint Assisted Living 063

Sun City Kumagaya - CCRC
サンシティ熊谷 - CCRC

既存施設の居住者の移転計画と併せて段階的に建設されたCCRC
A two-phased CCRC containing "Phase I" skilled nursing/assisted living and "Phase II" independent living apartments.

ダイニングや園芸、社交のための中庭（写真：松岡満男）
A protected courtyard for dining, gardening and socializtion (photo: Mitsuo Matsuoka)

サンシティ熊谷は1階の共用部で結ばれた2つの建物による終身介護施設で、「健常棟」(9階建てと6階建ての健常者用施設)と「パーソナルケア棟」(スキルドナーシング・認知症・介護施設)からなる。1階には、吹き抜けロビーやエクササイズルーム、大浴場、マージャン室、茶室、ダイニング、ジュース・カクテルバー、ライブラリー、工芸室からなる「コミュニティ」を有する、全ての介護レベルの居住者に対するアメニティがある。この階の廊下は、談話エリアや園芸ポットが配された庭を抱くようにある。

敷地には2棟の既存建物があったため、この建設は2期に分けて段階的に行われた。第1期のパーソナルケア棟は、既存のナーシングホームの居住者の新たな生活の場となり、第2期の健常棟は既存建物の解体後に建設された。

第1期の建物に隣接して公園があるのはこの計画の特異なところであり、その美観を楽しめるとともに居住者にとっての安らぎの場となっている。13床の認知症ユニットがあるパーソナルケア棟の1階には、安全な庭や居住者の知覚を刺激する多くのアクティビティがある。この建物は3層のナーシングユニットからなる「家」であり、各階では、オープンキッチンやガーデニング、アクティビティ、居間、浴室を持つ2組のエリアが形成されている。最上階の5階にはVIP用の特別室やリハビリテーション室、大きなルーフテラスがある。

健常棟にはさまざまな広さの居室や3層吹き抜けのロビー、主な共用諸室、屋外のパティオ、庭園などがある。

3層の吹き抜けのある健常棟のロビー（写真：松岡満男）
The lobby of the Independent Living Tower is a 3-story atrium (photo: Mitsuo Matsuoka)

This CCRC at Sun City Kumagaya is a full continuum of care with two buildings coupled by a common ground floor public level of common spaces: the "Independent Living Building" (9 stories and 6 stories of independent living) and the "Personal Care Building" (5 stories of skilled nursing, dementia and assisted living). The ground floor provides the "community" for the residents and houses amenities available to all inhabitants, regardless of care-level: atrium lobby, exercise, ofuro, mahjong, tea room, dining, juice and cocktail bars, library, art/activity room, etc. The single-loaded corridor serving this ground floor embraces a generous and protected garden with a mix of hard surface seating areas as well as raised planting beds.

The presence of two existing, outdated nursing facilities required that Sun City Kumagaya be constructed in two phases: Phase I is the Personal Care Building that became the new home for the existing nursing residents on the site. Phase II, the Independent Living Building, was constructed after the demolition of the outdated nursing buildings and added independent living apartments to the site.

A unique amenity to the site is the public park located adjacent to the Phase I building. This park, its openness and activity offer beauty as well as entertainment to these least-mobile residents. Within the Personal Care Building is a ground floor, highly designed 13-bed dementia unit with its own protected garden, and a number of activities intended to capture the residents with meaningful diversions. This building is the home of three floors of nursing units, each subdivided into two neighborhoods per floor and offering dining with open kitchens, gardening, activities, living room and bathing. The top floor, L5, offers VIP suites, rehab services and a large roof terrace for all CCRC residents.

The second phase, the IL Building, completed the CCRC with apartment units of various sizes. The three-story atrium lobby is located in this building as are the majority of common spaces and outdoor patios and gardens.

1階主廊下の小さなライブラリーと談話コーナー
（写真：松岡満男）
Small library and meeting place on ground floor Main Corridor (photo: Mitsuo Matsuoka)

中庭から見る介護棟（正面）と共用部（右）
A view to the Personal Care Building (backgorund) and common area (right) from the courtyard

Location: Kumagaya-shi, Kanagawa Japan
Completion: 2005
Site Area: 9,017.45 sqm
Gross Floor Area: 17,975 sqm
    7,175 sqm ("Personal Care Bldg")
    10,800 sqm ("Independent Living Bldg")
Height: "Personal Care Bldg" = 5 stories; "IL Bldg" = 9 stories and 6 stories
Structure: RC and Steel/Concrete structure
Number of Rooms:
    120 nursing and assisted living units
    100 independent living units
Parking: 50 surface spaces
Finishes:
<Predominant Exterior Wall>
    Tile and Glass
<Main lobby>
    Floor: Stone and Carpet
    Wall: Vinyl Wall Covering and Wood
    Ceiling: Gypsum Wallboard

Client: Half Century More Co., Ltd.
Architect for Schematic Design: Office of Dennis Cope / Architect
    (Dennis Copeand Kentaro Furuya, and Alan Bright of HOK)
Architect for Design Development: Kanko Kikaku Sekkeisha Co., Ltd.
Interior Designer for Skilled Nursing/Assisted Living "Personal Care Building":
    Graeber, Simmons & Cowan
    (Lea von Kaenel, IIDA and Pollyanna Little, IIDA)
Interior Designer for Independent Living Independent Living Building:
    Hirsch-Bedner Associates
    (Michael Sandler)
Landscape Designer: SWA Group/San Francisco
    (John Loomis, designer)
Predominant Contractor: Shimizukensetsu Co., Ltd

認知症ユニットの変化ある主廊下（写真：松岡満男）
The main street of the Dementia Unit is designed with a variety of diversions for these special residents (photo: Mitsuo Matsuoka)

この施設のいくつかの特徴。
- このキャンパスには全ての居住者の交流を促進し、物理的にも精神的にも居住者を刺激する安全な共用部がある。
- 1階にある13床の認知症ユニットでは、居住者の特殊なニーズに応ずるための設計上の工夫が施されている。広めの廊下は水槽やキオスク、ロッキングチェア、モック、キッチン、などがある変化に満ちた「アクティビティ・ストリート」となり、落ち着いた雰囲気のダイニング、庭や散策路へのアクセスがある。食事／リネンサービスは、ユニットでの往来が最小限となるように配されている。

Several features distinguish this facility:
- This campus offers a public level that is available and "owned" by all residents regardless of frailty. This encourages socialization and stimulates the residents physically and mentally, all within a secure environment.
- The 13-bed dementia unit on L1 contains a number of design features intended to address the special needs of these residents: the widened corridor becomes an "activity street" with various diversions (aquarium, kiosks, rocking chairs, mock kitchen), discreet dining, unencumbered outdoor access to enclosed garden and path, and dietary/linen services have been kept to the periphery of the unit to minimize outside traffic within the unit.

介護棟の1階廊下（写真：松岡満男）
Ground floor corridor of Personal Care Building
(photo: Mitsuo Matsuoka)

介護棟（第2期）の外観と公園に隣接する庭園
Exterior of Personal Care Building (Phase I) and protected garden adjacent to public park

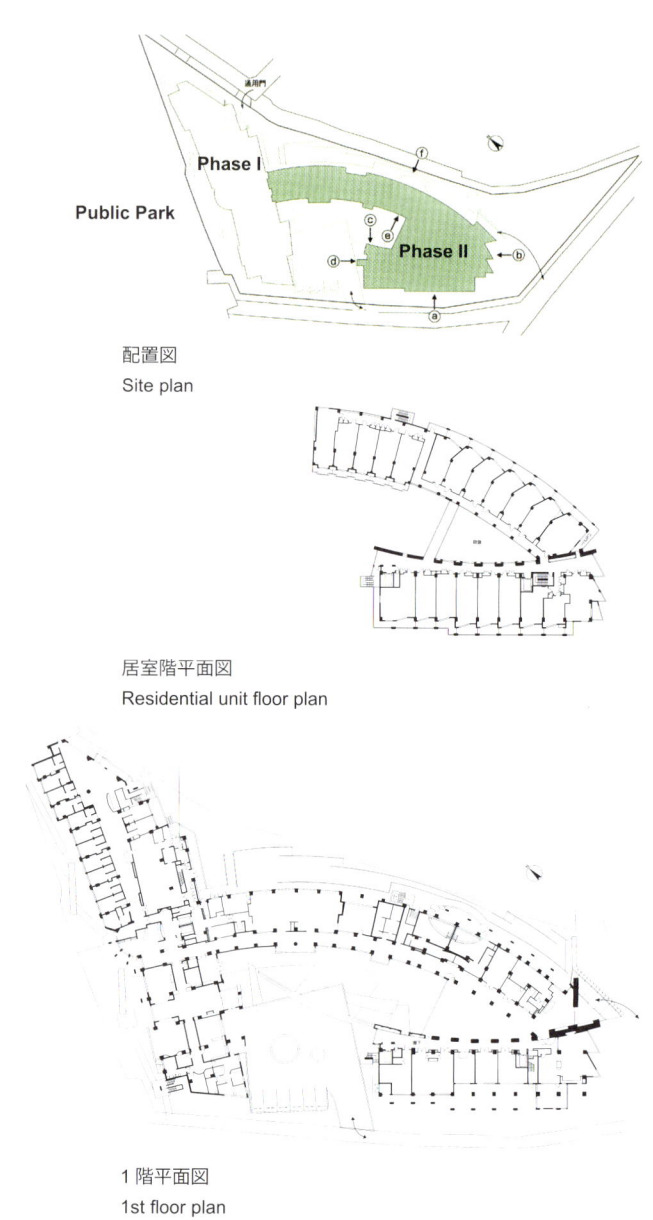

配置図
Site plan

居室階平面図
Residential unit floor plan

1階平面図
1st floor plan

健常者用居室平面図
Independet Living unit plan

自然を眺める大きな窓のある介護居室
（写真：松岡満男）
Skilled Nursing resident rooms have generous window areas to maximize contact with Nature (photo: Mitsuo Matsuoka)

ライブラリー（写真：松岡満男）
The library seating area (photo: Mitsuo Matsuoka)

2つの建物をつなぐ庭園脇の共用部の廊下
（写真：松岡満男）
The main corridor adjacent to the protected courtyard connects the two phases and is the "main street" for the CCRC common spaces
(photo: Mitsuo Matsuoka)

Essex & Sussex Hotel
エセックス&サセックスホテル

富裕なニューヨーカーの避暑施設の再生によるシニアアパートメント
Independent Living Facility Luxury Apartments – Rehabilitation of a summer playground for the very wealthy of New York and Philadelphia.

居住者用のフレンドリーな車寄せと玄関（写真：ボブ・ゴールデン・フォトグラフィ）
New Resident Friendly Entrance - Porte Cochere Entrance (photo: Bob Golden Photography)

400室のホテルとしてニュージャージー州北部の海岸に1941年に建てられたエセックス&サセックスは、巨大都市の日常的な刺激や騒音から逃避して、浜辺でのプライバシーや静けさを求めるニューヨークやフィラデルフィアの富裕層のための避暑施設の一部であった。かつて大統領が滞在したことや、『ラグタイム』や『グレート・ギャツビー』などの映画が撮影されたこともある。スプリングレイク湖と大西洋に挟まれたエセックス&サセックスでは、165室の豪華なアパートメントから勇壮なパノラマが展望できる。実績豊富なデベロッパーによるこのプロジェクトは、既存の建物を新しい健常高齢者施設のコミュニティへと転換するものであった。このかつての華麗な面影を残す建物の雰囲気を保つために、設計チームとニュージャージー州コミュニティ関連部局とが密接に戦略を検討した。

建物の西側の街路から居住者やビジターを迎える新しい表玄関と車寄せを配するために、敷地計画が見直された。メインウィング・ガーデンレベルとテラスレベルには共用部がある。メインウィングの西側の玄関では、ピアノラウンジに向けて2層分の吹き抜けが開かれている。既存の間仕切壁は取り除かれマルチメディア室やビリヤード室、カード室、インターネットラウンジ、化粧室へと様変わりした。以前のボールルームは歴史性を重んじたメイン・ダイニングルームへと改修された。

エセックス&サセックスは、リゾートならではのスケールやディテールを用いて、豪華さとともに元の建物のビクトリア調の造りなどを想い起こさせる海辺の「王冠」となって蘇った。

大西洋からの航空写真（写真：ザ・アプライド・カンパニーズ）
Arial View from Atlantic Ocean (photo: The Applied Companies)

The Essex & Sussex was constructed in 1914 on the northern coast of New Jersey as a 400-room hotel. It was part of a summer playground for the very wealthy of New York and Philadelphia seeking the privacy of the beachfront and a quiet getaway from the sights and sounds that a giant city brings to everyday living. Legend has it that more than one U.S. President stayed at the hotel, and movies such as Ragtime and The Great Gatsby were filmed there. Nestled between Spring Lake and the Atlantic Ocean, Essex & Sussex provides spectacular panoramas for the retirees who live in its 165 luxury apartments. This project for a well-established developer consists of the conversion of the existing structure into a new independent senior housing community. The design team worked closely with the New Jersey Department of Community Affairs in developing a strategy to retain the ambience of this once-glorious building.

The site plan was reconfigured for a new Main Entry and Porte Cochere on the west side of the building, with resident and visitor access at street level. The Main Wing Garden Level and Terrace Level contain the community spaces for the facility. On the west side of the Main Wing, the new entrance was opened to a two-story atrium directly off of the Piano Lounge. Existing partitions were removed and reconfigured for a Multimedia Room, Billiard Room, Card Room, Internet Lounge, and new Restrooms. The former Ballroom was historically restored into the Main Dining Room.

Every effort was taken to recall the resort"s scale, detailing, and grandeur, and the original structure's fabled Victorian elegance. The Essex & Sussex has once again become the ""Crown Jewel"" of the seashore.

Client: The Applied Companies, Hoboken, New Jersey
Architect for Schematic Design: Kanalstein Danton Associates, P.A.
Architect for Design Development: Kanalstein Danton Associates, P.A.
Interior Designer: Merlino Design Partnership, Inc.
Predominant Contractor: A.J.D. Construction Company

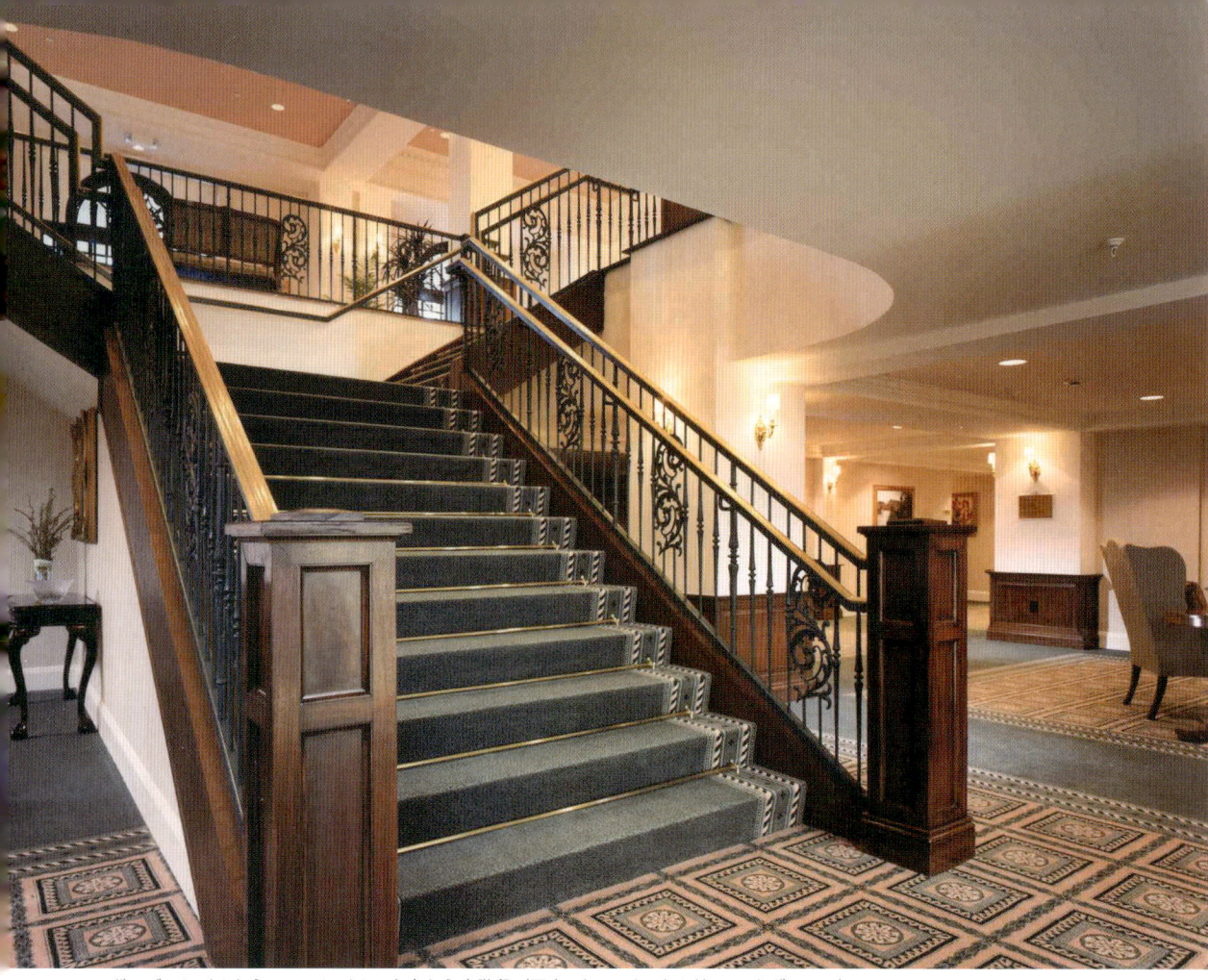

ガーデンレベルからテラスレベルへと向かう大階段（写真：トム・ベルナルド・フォトグラフィ）
Grand Staircase leading to Terrace Level - Garden Level (photo: Tom Bernard Photography)

テラスレベルのギャラリー（写真：トム・ベルナルド・フォトグラフィ）
Gallery - Terrace Level (photo: Tom Bernard Photography)

1914年のビクトリアン・バーのあるピアノラウンジとバー
（写真：トム・ベルナルド・フォトグラフィ）
Piano Lounge & Bar with "1914" Victorian Bar - Terrace Level (photo: Tom Bernard Photography)

ガーデンレベルへの大階段（写真：トム・ベルナルド・フォトグラフィ）
Grand Staircase leading down to Garden Level
(photo: Tom Bernard Photography)

スプリングレイク湖から望む外観（写真：ボブ・ゴールデン・フォトグラフィ）
Lakeside Exterior View looking East over Spring Lake (photo: Bob Golden Photography)

エセックス & サセックスは、ニュージャージー州の再生規則を適用した、同州では最初の主要な再生プロジェクトである。ニュージャージー州コミュニティ関係部局によるこの規則は、この建物のような木造の既存建物の再生や改修のためのガイドラインである。

The Essex & Sussex is the first major rehabilitation project completed in New Jersey using the newly adopted New Jersey - Rehabilitation Code. This code adopted by the New Jersey Department of Community Affairs (DCA) allows for the reconstruction and alteration of existing wood frame structure, within the restrictive guidelines set up specifically for this type of structure and the preservation of like structures.

Location: Spring Lake, New Jersey U.S.A.
Completion: 2003
Site Area: 13,440 sqm
Gross Floor Area: 18,370 sqm
Height: 6 stories
Structure: Steel and Concrete structure
Number of Rooms: 165 apartments
Parking: Valet Parking
Finishes:
<Predominant Exterior Wall>
　　　Brick, Stucco, Wood Trim and Asphalt Shingle Roof
<Main lobby>
　　　Floor: Marble Tile with Custom Area Rugs
　　　Wall: Plaster Walls with Ornamental Trim
　　　Ceiling: Plaster Ceiling with Ornamental Trim
Award: Building Design & Construction Magazine, 19th annual Reconstruction Awards, Essex & Sussex, Spring Lake, New Jersey, October 2002; Seniors Housing Council, 2003 Best of Seniors Housing Design Awards, Essex & Sussex, Spring Lake, New Jersey, Service-Enriched Housing

有名なボールルームを改修したテラスレベルのメイン・ダイニングルーム（写真：トム・ベルナルド・フォトグラフィ）
Famed Ball Room - Now Main Dining Room - Terrace Level (photo: Tom Bernard Photography)

ガーデンレベルの吹き抜けと表玄関
（写真：トム・ベルナルド・フォトグラフィ）
New Atrium Addition & main resident entrance
- Garden Level
(photo: Tom Bernard Photography)

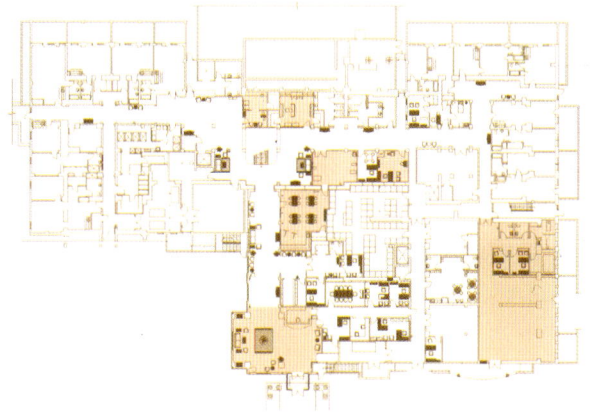

ガーデンフロア平面図
Garden floor plan

テラスレベルのプライベート・ダイニングルーム（写真：トム・ベルナルド・フォトグラフィ）
Private Dining Room - Terrace Level (photo: Tom Bernard Photography)

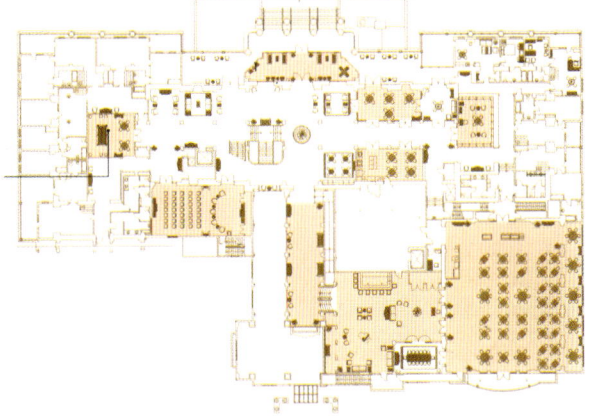

1階平面図
1st floor plan

ガーデンレベルのメインロビーとコンシェルジェデスク
（写真：トム・ベルナルド・フォトグラフィ）
New Lobby Addition & Concierge Desk - Garden Level
(photo: Tom Bernard Photography)

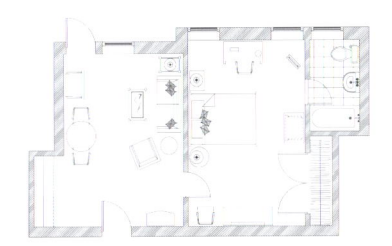

ワンベッドルーム平面図
One bedroom plan

大西洋を望むテラスレベルの日光浴室（写真：トム・ベルナルド・フォトグラフィ）
Solarium overlooking Atlantic Ocean - Terrace Level (photo: Tom Bernard Photography)

オーシャンビューのあるモデルルーム（写真：トム・ベルナルド・フォトグラフィ）
Ocean View Model Apartment (photo: Tom Bernard Photography)

居住部の標準的な廊下（写真：トム・ベルナルド・フォトグラフィ）
Typical Residential Corridor (photo: Tom Bernard Photography)

Essex & Sussex Hotel 075

Sacravia Seijo
サクラビア成城

豪華な設備と充実したサービスを誇る高齢者の住まい
An elderly housing with prestigious facilities and services.

庭園から見るダイニングルーム
Dining room view from garden

サクラビア成城は東京の都心から私鉄急行で15分の駅前の北、桜並木のある閑静な高級住宅街に居を構える。

敷地の周囲の街路に沿って流れるせせらぎを渡り、ポータルを通り抜けると緑豊かなアプローチの向こうに、深い車寄せのキャノピーがある館が見える。ゆったりとしたボリュームに古典的な装飾を加えた外観、高級木材で仕上げられた受付ロビー、そしてそこに置かれたオリジナルの美術品がこの施設のハードとソフト面の本格性を物語っている。

大きなガラス窓から庭を望むゴージャスなダイニングルームは、ローズカラーを基調としており、そのサービスはホテルを凌ぐものである。バンケットホール、シアター、娯楽室、アトリエ、トレーニングルーム、理美容室などでは、ブランド力を活かしたハイレベルな運営が行われている。

The Sacravia Seijo is located in the high-income residential area with Sakura trees, fifteen minutes express train ride from downtown of Tokyo.
Residents access the entry with a large canopy through a bridge with a portal on a stream sounding the site. The volume of building, exterior wall with classic element, a lobby finished by high grade natural wood and original fine arts tell authenticity of facility and operation.

Gorgeous rose color dining room with the wide window extends to a stylish garden. Services at there is far beyond that at hotels. High-level professional services are provided at banquet hall, theatre, hobby room, atelier, training room, beauty saloon and other areas.

桜の杜の中に展開する施設
Building within forest of Sakura trees

Client: Primestage Co., Ltd.
Architect for Schematic Design: Takenaka Corporation
Architect for Design Development: Takenaka Corporation
Predominant Contractor: Takenaka Corporation

Location: Setagaya-ku, Tokyo JAPAN
Completion: 1988
Renovation/Extension: 2004
Site Area: 9,972 sqm
Gross Floor Area: 22,403 sqm
Height: Under ground 1 story; Above ground 10 stories
Structure: Steel and Reinforced Concrete structure
Number of Rooms: 150 rooms
Parking: 43 cars
Finishes:
<Predominant Exterior Wall>
　　　Ceramic Tile
<Main lobby>
　　　Floor: Wood
　　　Wall: Wood
　　　Ceiling: Plaster Board/EP

窓越しに庭園を望む、ローズカラーを基調としたダイニングルーム
Dining room finished with rose color viewing garden

オリジナルの美術品が置かれた受付ロビー
Reception lobby housing original arts

最上階に設けられたスカイラウンジ
Sky lounge at the top floor

サクラビア成城は東京都世田谷区成城にある、日本でも有数の充実した設備とサービスを誇る60歳からの終身利用権方式の住まいである。ホームセキュリティと在宅医療のエキスパートであるセコム株式会社と快適な住環境を創造する森ビル株式会社が共同出資で設立した株式会社プライムステージが運営している。「生涯安心」をテーマに各種生活サービスを極めて高いレベルで提供している。

The Sacravia Seijo, located at Seijo town in Setagaya Ward of Tokyo, is long term care home for over 60 preparing prestigious facilities and services. This is operated by Primestage Co., Ltd., a joint invested by Secom Co., Ltd., expert in serving both home security and home medical care, and Mori Building Co., Ltd., expert in development of comfortable places for habitation. We provide various life services to live at ease at an extremely high level through life.

緑に囲まれたアプローチと玄関
Approach with green

緑に囲まれたアプローチの夕景
Approach at evening on the green

さまざまに使用される多目的ホール
Multi functional room for various activities

クリニックの受付
Reception of clinic

マージャン室
Mah-jong room

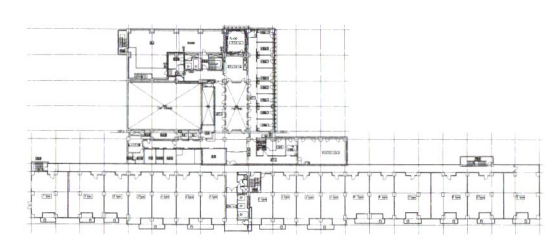

居室階平面図
Residents room floor plan

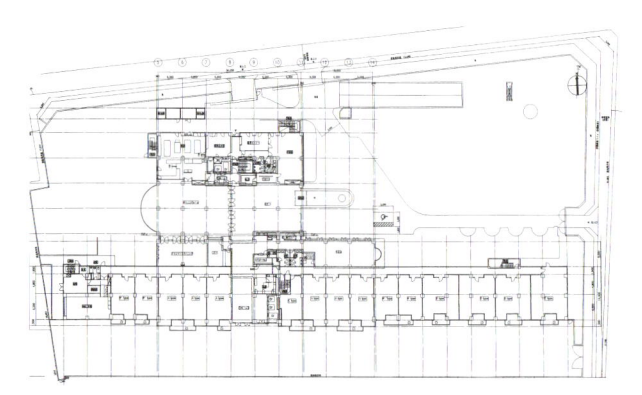

シアター
Theatre

1階平面図
1st floor plan

ワンベッドルームの居間
Living room in one bed room

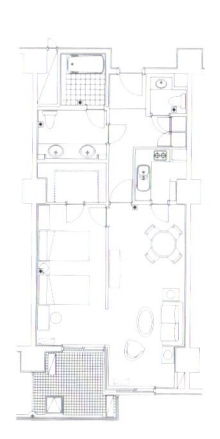

居室平面図
Unit plan

広いバルコニーに続くベッドルーム
Bedroom expanding to large balcony

サクラビア成城 081

The Tradition of the Palm Beaches

ザ・トラディション・パームビーチ

徹底したマーケット調査で導き出された高齢者施設の新しいタイプ
A new model by blending services, housing, and programs focused on an older population with clear consumer demands for choice and options.

湖越しに見る建物の夕景（写真：マゼリー・フォトグラフィ）
Exterior Evening Across Lake (photo: Massery Photography)

Client: Marilyn and Stanley M. Katz Seniors Campus
Master Designer: Perkins Eastman
Architect for Schematic Design: Perkins Eastman
Architect for Design Development: Perkins Eastman
Interior Designer: Perkins Eastman
Landscape Designer: Cotleur & Hearing
Predominant Contractor: The Whiting-Turner Company

湖側に張り出した屋外のパティオ（写真：マゼリー・フォトグラフィ）
Exterior Patio (photo: Massery Photography)

　ザ・トラディション・パームビーチは、介護付き居住サービスとハウジング、および超高齢者(85歳以上)のための選択に幅のあるコミュニティのプログラムなどを融合した、高齢者施設の新しいモデルケースである。革新的な南フロリダのスポンサーによるザ・トラディションは、既存の長期介護型のキャンパスにハウジングとサービスを加えることで、より充実した施設群へと進化を遂げている。伝統的なCCRCを展開することは容易だが、このスポンサーはマーケットによく耳を傾けユニークなものを創ろうとした。

　マーケット調査によれば、満足な人生を送ってきた高齢者が、施設のサービス内容や形態に多様性を求めていることが判った。カスタマーが、現在居住している施設のサービスや、介護付きの新しいハウジング、より充実したサービスなどに選択の幅を求めていることは確かである。また、エクイティ(コンドミニアム)や基金(入居費)型でなく、「使った分だけ支払うシステム」や借家形式などの、より柔軟な経済的モデルを求めていることも明らかになった。

　ミズナーやブレーカーズホテルなど、南フロリダの伝統的で優雅な「グランドホテル」の現代版であることを、全体的なデザインコンセプトとした。上品なもてなしと快適な居住性を確保するために、スタッコのアーチやクレイタイルのベランダ、心地良い中庭などによってインテリアがつくられている。大理石のタイルが貼られたプロムナードからは、ダイニングやビストロ・カフェ、フィットネス、プールへと向かうことができる。

The Tradition of the Palm Beaches establishes a new model by blending assisted living services, housing, and community-based programs focused on an older population (85+) with clear consumer demands for choice and options. Sponsored by a progressive faith-based South Florida organization, The Tradition expands an existing long term care campus into a full continuum of housing and services. It would have been easy to develop a traditional continuing care retirement community, but the sponsor listened to its market and found a unique opportunity

The market study identified an older consumer that was aging successfully, but who found the coordination of services to be an increasing challenge. It was clear that this consumer wanted choices: services where they currently resided or new housing with "assistance in living" or a more sheltered full-service assisted living setting. It was also clear that the consumer desired a more flexible financial model with "pay as you go" services and rental housing, not equity (condominium) or endowment (entry fee) models.

The overall design concept resulted in a contemporary version of gracious "grand hotel" living in the South Florida tradition of the Mizners and the Breakers Hotel. Stucco arches, clay tiled verandas, and intimate courtyards give way to interiors that express genteel hospitality and comfortable residential living. The marble tiled promenade links the community with dining options, bistro/cafe, library, fitness and swimming pool.

サービスのしやすさのために、健常者用居室と介護居室とを並べて配した。各ウィングは独自のアイデンティティを有する一方、1階のダイニングや居間がウェルネスやスパ、レクレーション施設でつながっている。またこれらのエリアは、敷地内の居住者やコミュニティの関係者等によるアクセスを容易にするために、高齢者クリニックセンターとも結ばれている。

90日で100%の入居率を達成したことで、ザ・トラディションの成功は明らかであるが、それよりも（たぶん）柔軟性や選択性、丁重さをもってカスタマーに応える新しいモデルを確立したことが大きな成果である。

The design links residential living horizontally to assisted living for easy distribution of services. While each wing has its own identity, dining and living spaces are linked on the first floor through wellness, activity, spa, and recreational opportunities. These areas are in turn linked to a geriatric and clinic services center for easy access by on-site residents and community-at-large participants. Careful and sensitive zoning of the site and building allows several communities to "co-exist" with flexible and economically delivered services.

The Tradition's success can be measured by its achieving 100% occupancy in 90 days, but (perhaps) more importantly it successfully established a new model that responds to consumers with flexibility, choice, and graciousness.

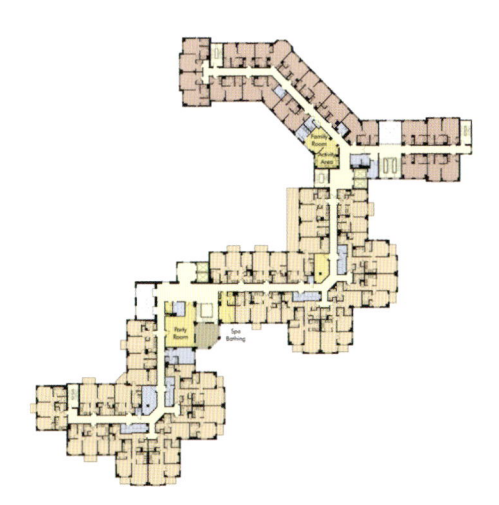

居室の居間（写真：マゼリー・フォトグラフィ）
Interior Resident Living Room (photo: Massery Photography)

2階平面図
2nd floor plan

配置図
Site plan

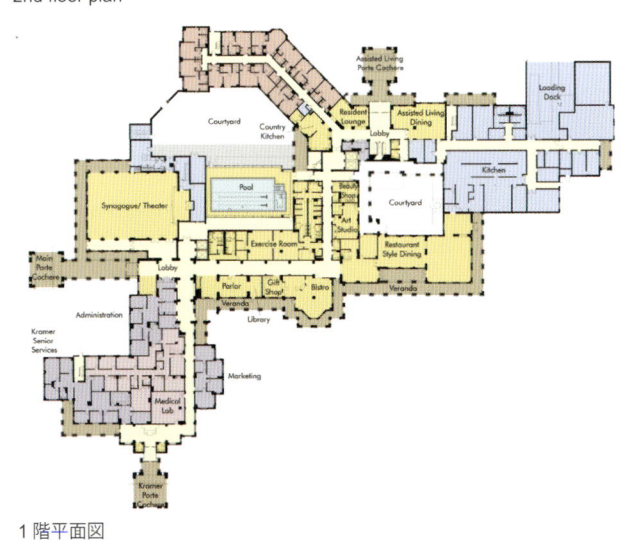

1階平面図
1st floor plan

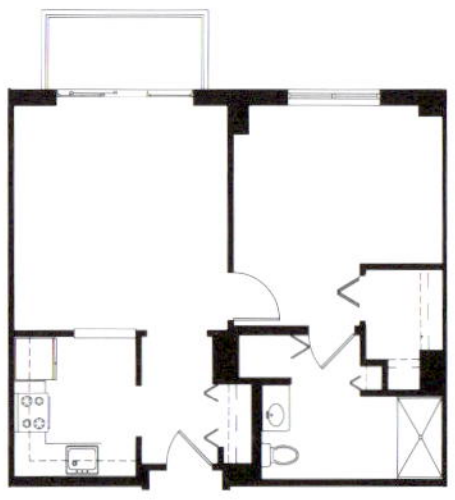

居室平面図
Unit plan

Location: West Palm Beach, FL U.S.A.
Completion: 2004
Site Area: 101,200 sqm
Gross Floor Area: 36,670 sqm
Height: 6 stories
Structure: Tensioned Core Structural System
Number of Rooms: 144 rooms
Parking: 482 cars
Finishes:
<Predominant Exterior Wall>
    Stucco
<Main lobby>
    Floor: Marble
    Wall: Paint/VWC on GWB
    Ceiling: GWB/ACT
Award: 2006 American Institute of Architects Design for Aging Award, Notable Project; 2006 Best of Seniors Housing Award, National Association of Home Builders 50+ Housing Council, Continuing Care Retirement Community - Overall Community: Small and Midsize

落ち着ける共用部の居間（写真：マゼリー・フォトグラフィ）
Interior Living Room (photo: Massery Photography)

このキャンパスには、以下のプログラム上のソリューションが含まれている。

- 訓練、評価、ホームヘルス、在宅の高齢者のための訪問介護サービスなどのある老人病サービスセンター
- ウェルネスと居住の継続性（入居時の平均は 85 歳）を提供する、アパートメントウィング形式の 102 ユニットの認定介護付居住施設
- 体が弱い居住者に、より包括的なサービスと安心を提供する 42 ユニットの介護付居住施設ウィング

The programmatic solution is a rich campus with a single structure that houses:

- a geriatric services center with training, assessment, home health and "out patient" services reaching at-home seniors.
- a 102-unit assisted living licensed residential apartment wing focused on wellness and aging-in-place (average age of entry 85)
- a 42-unit assisted living wing providing more comprehensive services and shelter for frail residents

家族で調理ができる広さと設備、雰囲気のあるファミリーキッチン（写真：マゼリー・フォトグラフィ）
Interior Family Kitchen (photo: Massery Photography)

Givens Estates

ギヴンズ・エステート

ノースカリフォルニアの美しい景観を活かした終身介護施設の増改築
CCRC expansion and renovation, located in the scenic mountains of North Carolina.

共用部の大廊下（写真：リオン・リッゾ、クリエイティブ・ソーシス・フォトグラフィ・インク）
Main corridor in common area (photo: Rion Rizzo, Creative Sources Photography, Inc.)

設計チームは、丘陵地特有の起伏を活かしながら、敷地から見える美しい山並みの景観を取り込むよう計画に配慮した。また、今回の増築棟の下を流れていた地下水流を設計に活かした。ダイニングテラスとウェルネスセンターのテラスとの間の地面に流れを配することで、この本質的に不利な要素をアメニティへと変換した。それは居住部や共用部から見える静かな池へと向かって、屋外の斜面を流れ下る。

このプロジェクトは築20年の既存建物に接している。運営の効率性と居住者の利便性を高めるために、増築部分と既存部分の機能が再整理された他、アッシュビル地方の歴史性に呼応する住宅の美しさを反映しながら既存部分が改築された。

新しいアパート棟の住戸や屋外の共用部からのピスガー山脈への眺めなど、ここでの景観の美しさが最大限に活かされている。さらに居住者が屋外での時間を楽しめるように、歩道や森の散策路などのさまざまな小道を効果的に配している。

建物背面の外観（写真：ビリー・シムコックス、フリーマンホワイト・インク）
Rear view of the building (photo: Billy Simcox, FreemanWhite, Inc.)

Client: Givens Estates
Master Designer: FreemanWhite, Inc.
Architect for Schematic Design: FreemanWhite, Inc.
Architect for Design Development: FreemanWhite, Inc.
Interior Designer: GMK Interiors
Landscape Designer: Melrose & Associates
Predominant Contractor: Rodgers Builders

For this facility, the design team worked to create a plan that would take advantage of the difficulty, hilly site's beautiful mountain views, while working within the constraints of the terrain. The design incorporates an existing underground stream that flowed beneath the planned expansion. Turning a potential liability into an amenity, designers brought it to the surface between the main dining terrace and the Wellness Center terrace. Its path then tumbles down an adjacent landscaped slope to a quiet pond viewed from both residential and commons spaces.

FreemanWhite's project connects to an existing, 20-year-old building. The new expansion spaces are integrated into the existing spaces to maximize operational efficiencies and residence convenience, and the existing institutional spaces were updated to reflect a residential aesthetic that responds to the rich heritage of the Asheville region.

Taking advantage of the scenic environment, the new apartment building also maximizes resident views of the surrounding Pisgah Mountains from both apartments and public exterior gathering spaces. Additionally, the project integrates numerous pedestrian paths, ranging from paved walks to forest trails, maintaining a tradition of resident connection to the environment.

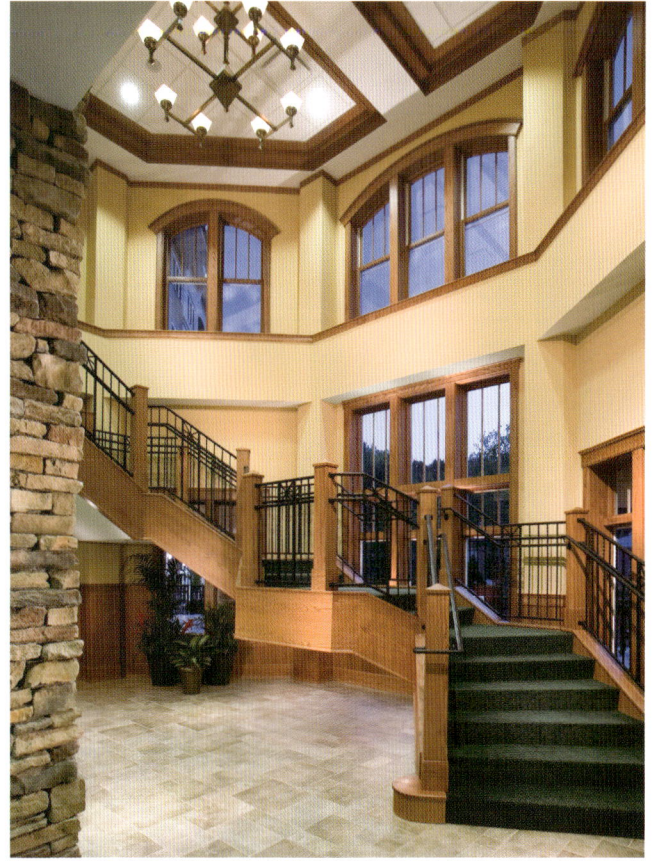

大階段
（写真：リオン・リッゾ、クリエイティブ・ソーシス・フォトグラフィ・インク）
Main stair way (photo: Rion Rizzo, Creative Sources Photography, Inc.)

建物正面の外観（写真：ビリー・シムコックス、フリーマンホワイト・インク）
Front view of the building (photo: Billy Simcox, FreemanWhite, Inc.)

配置図
Site plan

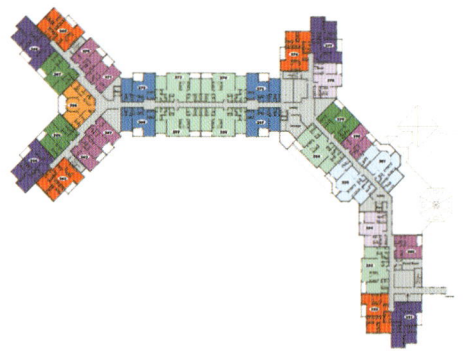

2階平面図
2nd floor plan

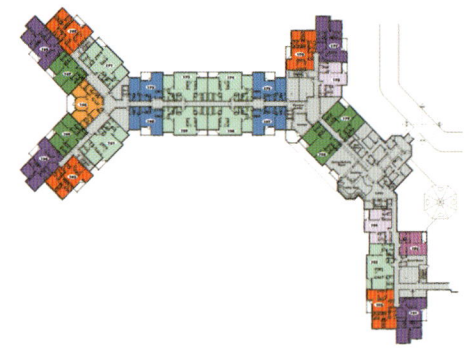

1階平面図
1st floor plan

居室平面図
Unit plan

Location: Asheville, North Carolina U.S.A.
Completion: 2005
Renovation/Extension: 2005
Site Area: 171,180 sqm
Gross Floor Area: 46,660 sqm
Height: 5 stories
Structure: Steel structure
Number of Rooms:
 59 cottages
 137 apartments
 (25 new studio units, 92 two bedroom + den units)

Parking:
 225 cars in open parking lots
 75 cars in underground garage
Finishes:
<Predominant Exterior Wall>
 Brick and Stone
<Main lobby>
 Floor: Carpet and Wood
 Wall: Vinyl Wall Covering and Paint
 Ceiling: GWB and Acoustical Panels

コモンズエリア（写真：リオン・リッゾ、クリエイティブ・ソーシス・フォトグラフィ・インク）
Commons area (photo: Rion Rizzo, Creative Sources Photography, Inc.)

ギヴンズ・エステートによって最初に示されたプログラムは、従来の一般的なプログラムからはかなり逸脱していた。このプロジェクトでは、多くのコモンプログラムを新築の建物に移設・集中化し、居住者がそこへ至るまでの移動距離を短縮している。

Many of the existing program spaces were inadequate for the numerous programs offered by Givens Estates. FreemanWhite's project relocated many of these spaces into a new building, centralizing the "common" program functions and minimizing the travel distance to these daily functions for a majority of residents.

ウェルネスセンターのプール
（写真：リオン・リッゾ、クリエイティブ・ソーシス・フォトグラフィ・インク）
Pool in wellness center (photo: Rion Rizzo, Creative Sources Photography, Inc.)

メイン・ダイニングルーム
（写真：リオン・リッゾ、クリエイティブ・ソーシス・フォトグラフィ・インク）
Main dining room (photo: Rion Rizzo, Creative Sources Photography, Inc.)

Givens Estates 089

Aldersgate Continuing Care Retirement Community
エルダーズゲート終身介護施設

競争市場で勝ち抜くための戦略的な改善を施す終身介護施設
CCRC repositioning, renovation and expansion to increase visibility in a competitive market; includes an innovative 45-bed Alzheimer's unit.

競合する他の施設との競争が日増しに激しくなってきたこの既存の高齢者コミュニティでは、長期にわたる戦略的な将来計画を立てるために、設計者は既存敷地の再開発やコミュニティの移設など、いくつかのオプションを検討した。フリーマン・ホワイトはワークショップを通して、将来の成功のために施設を完全なものにするためのさまざまな物理的および経済的課題に取り組んだ。新たなマスタープランは既存のキャンパスを刷新した。居住者やビジターは、コテージコミュニティを通り過ぎ、既存の湖を渡って新しい「タウンスクエア」へと向かう新たな進入路を利用する。タウンスクエアはコミュニティ棟と健常棟に囲まれている。45床のメモリーサポート・ユニットは中央コミュニティ棟に隣接している。

このコミュニティは、居間や会議室、屋内プール、ウェルネスセンター、銀行、ライブラリー、管理事務所などからなるコミュニティ棟に加え、60ユニットのアパート棟を含んでいる。メモリーサポート・ユニットは、オープンスペースや1920年代のアクティビティを想い起こさせる広場の周りに配される15室からなる3つのエリアからなる。

メモリーサポート・ユニットは、記憶障害のある高齢者のために「エデン・オルタナティブ」から派生した「メインストリートUSAコンセプト」の考え方を全般的に導入しており、居住者やスタッフ、家族、コミュニティ同士の積極的なふれあいを促進している。そこには、居住者がアクティビティに参加したり見たりすることのできるライフスキル・ステーションを発展させた散策路がある。居住者は住居やビレッジの敷地内を、朝から晩まで自由に動き回ることができる。

メモリーサポート・タウンスクエア（写真：ティム・ブックマン）
View of Memory Support Town Square (photo: Tim Buchman)

共用棟の外観（写真：ティム・ミューラー）
Exterior View of Commons (photo: Tim Mueller)

Client: United Methodist Retirement Communities
Master Designer: FreemanWhite, Inc.
Architect for Schematic Design: FreemanWhite, Inc.
Architect for Design Development: FreemanWhite, Inc.
Interior Designer: FreemanWhite, Inc.
Landscape Designer: Site Solutions
Predominant Contractor: Bovis Lend Lease

In developing a long-range, strategic plan for this existing retirement community that was finding it increasingly difficult to compete against newer facilities, designers evaluated options for redeveloping the existing site or relocating the community. Through a series of workshops, FreemanWhite addressed various physical and financial issues to reposition the facility for future success. A new master plan completely reinvented the existing campus, and a new entrance road brings residents and visitors past a new cottage community and across an existing lake to the new "town square". The town square is bordered by a new community building and independent living apartment building. A new, 45-bed memory support unit is connected to the central community building.

The community includes a new 60-unit apartment building, as well as a community building containing living areas, meeting rooms, an indoor pool and wellness center, bank, library, and administrative offices. The memory support unit includes three, 15-resident "neighborhoods" located around a square that recalls the open spaces and activities of a 1920's town.

The memory support unit incorporates the "EDEN ALTERNATIVE" philosophy and Main Street USA Concepts into a holistic environment for seniors with memory impairment that promotes positive interaction among residents, staff, families, and the community. Its design features expanded life skill stations where residents are able to participate in or observe activities, providing what the staff calls "Purposeful Pathways" throughout the village. From morning until bedtime, the residents are free to move throughout all areas of their household and village.

共用棟と散策路（写真：ティム・ブックマン）
Exterior Drive of Commons Building (photo: Tim Buchman)

Aldersgate Continuing Care Retirement Community

共用棟のカフェダイニング（写真：ティム・ブックマン）
Cafe Dining in Commons building (photo: Tim Buchman)

共用棟の多目的チャペル（写真：ティム・ブックマン）
Multi-purpose / Chapel in Commons building (photo: Tim Buchman)

共用棟の居間（写真：ティム・ブックマン）
Living room in Commons building (photo: Tim Buchman)

「エデン・オルタナティブ」の哲学

米国では1990年代まで、ナーシングホームは衛生的だが無味乾燥な雰囲気で、高齢者の治療のための病院のようであった。そこでウィリアム・H・トーマス博士は、健康上の問題よりも高齢者の身体能力や尊厳、生活の質を重視した介護哲学をうちたてた。博士は、孤独、無力感、退屈をナーシングホームにおける3つの社会的問題であると定義した。それで彼は、子供や動植物との触れ合いを通して居住者に生活の目的意識を持たせ、アクティビティを促しながらより快適な家庭のような環境を提供することで、生活環境の質の向上を目指した。植物や大切にしていた物で満たされている明るい雰囲気の住居で、高齢者は動植物の世話をしたり元気な子供達と接することができる。

"Eden Alternative" Philosophy

Until the 1990's, in the United States, nursing homes were assumed to be similar to hospitals, a place to be very sanitized and sterile and focused on providing treatment of a resident's illness. Dr. William H. Thomas, MD developed a philosophy of care that focuses on a resident's strengths, dignity, and quality of life rather than just treating health problems. Dr. Thomas recognized and defined the three social problem areas within nursing homes – loneliness, helplessness and boredom. He then developed an approach to creating better quality environments for seniors by bringing in children, plants and pets to provide residents with a sense of purpose in life, stimulating activities and comfortable more homelike environments. The resident's care for the pets and the plants and interact with the children watching them play and interacting with them in activities, while living in an households that are filled with light, plants and cherished items from there life experiences.

健常棟の外観（写真：ティム・ミューラー）
Exterior View of IL Apartment Building (photo: Tim Mueller)

ウェルネスセンターのプール（写真：ティム・ブックマン）
Pool in wellness center (photo: Tim Buchman)

メモリーサポート・エリアのコートヤード（写真：ティム・ブックマン）
Courtyard of Memory Support Area (photo: Tim Buchman)

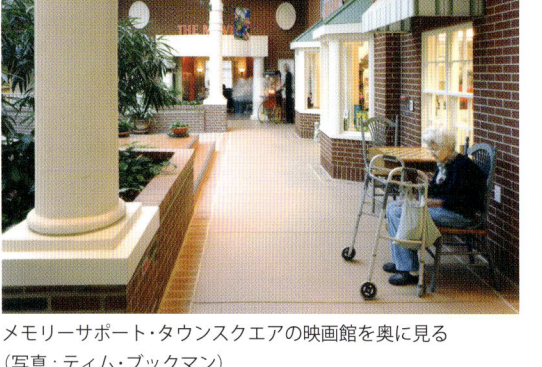

記憶障害を持つ高齢者のための総合的な居住環境を創る上で、介護環境が周辺と積極的に係わり合うことができるように努めた。例えば、外部への容易なアクセスや、中心的な要素であるタウンスクエアからの、薄く色のかかった大きなスカイライトを通した空への眺めである。

In creating a holistic living environment for seniors with memory impairment, this design of an independent, caring environment facilitates a positive interactive with the surroundings. It encourages easy access to the outside, and its chief organizing element - the town square - allows views to the sky through a large, tinted skylight.

メモリーサポート・タウンスクエアの映画館を奥に見る
(写真:ティム・ブックマン)
View to Cinema in Memory Support Town Square
(photo: Tim Buchman)

住戸の居間（写真:ティム・ブックマン）
Apart Living (photo: Tim Buchman)

住戸のダイニング（写真:ティム・ブックマン）
Apart Dining (photo: Tim Buchman)

配置図
Site plan

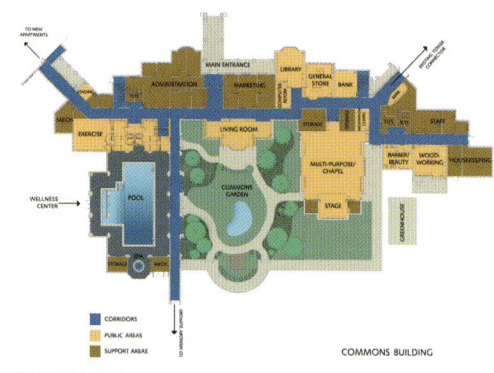

共用棟平面図
Community floor plan

居室平面図
Unit plan

メモリー・ユニット平面図
Memory unit floor plan

Location: Charlotte, North Carolina U.S.A
Completion: 2002
Renovation/Extension: 2002
Site Area: 13,910 sqm for Memory Support Unit
Gross Floor Area: 17,470 sqm
Height: 2-3 above ground stories main building / 8-9 apartment building
Structure: Predominately wood frame
Number of Rooms:
    197 apartments
    104 skilled care beds,
    56 cottages
    45 Alzheimer's units
    27 assisted living units
Parking: 373 cars in open surface lots
Finishes:
<Predominant Exterior Wall>
    Brick with Horizontal Aluminum Siding
<Main lobby>
    Floor: Carpet
    Wall: Vinyl Wall Covering and Paint
    Ceiling: GWB and Acoustical Panels
Award: AIA/AAHSA Design for Aging Review, 2001; Design 2001: Nursing Homes (LTCM), Best in Category: Architecture and Interiors
(Project in Progress)

第三章
地域性への配慮にこだわった
地域密着型

Chapter Three
***Reflected
Locality***

Maravilla

マラヴィラ

サンタバーバラのスパニッシュコロニアル・スタイルによる豪華施設
A luxury CCRC that integrates seamlessly with Santa Barbara's Spanish Colonial Architecture.

プールとシニアセンター。テラスには暖炉がある（写真：アーキテクチュラル・フォトグラフィ・インク）
Pool and Senior Center (photo: www.architecturephotoinc.com)

サンタバーバラの北のサンタヤネツ山脈の麓に抱かれたマラヴィラは、浜辺や巨大なショッピングセンター、主要幹線道路、空港に近接しており、さまざまな意味で利便性に恵まれている。施設は量感を和らげたり動線を明解にするためのウィングや中庭から構成されており、またコミュニティへの親しみやすさや住宅のスケール感をそなえている。アーチ型の窓や出入口、バルコニー、クレイタイルの屋根、トレリス、キューポラ、中庭などの使用によって、この地域の伝統的なスパニッシュコロニアル・スタイルの特徴を表現している。ずっと前からそこにあったような感じを出すために、さまざまなファサードやディテールが使われている。それぞれの中庭は、地域の植栽や個性的なデザインによって豊かにランドスケープされている。マラヴィラはそのどこをとっても入念にデザインを凝らしている。階段と噴水には地域のクラフトタイルが貼られている。また、手の込んだ錬鉄のディテールがある外部扉の多くは特注品である。表玄関や屋外の炉辺は地域の砂岩でできている。マラヴィラは、集合住宅への法的制約があるこの地域で創られた、過去30年間では最初の大型シニアハウジング・コミュニティである。

Nestled at the base of the Santa Ynez Mountains just north of Santa Barbara, Maravilla is close to the beach, expansive shopping centers, major freeways and the local airport. It takes full advantage of the region's vast resources. To provide the community with an intimate, residential-scale look and feel, the building footprint has numerous finger branches and courtyards to "break up" exterior mass and improve circulation. The design complements the region's classic Spanish colonial vernacular with abundant use of arched windows and doorways, balconies, clay tile roofs, trellises, cupolas and courtyards. The facades and design details are varied, giving the community a growth over time feel. Landscaping makes use of a wide palette of native vegetation, with each courtyard containing different species and design treatments. Maravilla is consistent in its superior, amenity rich design. Stairways and fountains are adorned with locally crafted tile. Many exterior doors are hand-hewn with wrought iron detail. The main entry gate and outdoor fireplace are constructed with native sandstone. Because of severe municipal restrictions on multifamily construction, Maravilla is the first large-scale senior housing community to be built in the region in more than 30 years.

健常棟のロビー（写真：アーキテクチュラル・フォトグラフィ・インク）
Independent Living Lobby (photo: www.architecturephotoinc.com)

健常棟のダイニングルーム（写真：アーキテクチュラル・フォトグラフィ・インク）
Independent Living Dining Room (photo: www.architecturephotoinc.com)

配置図
Site plan

Client: Senior Resource Group, LLC
Master Designer: Mithun and Cearnal Andrulaitis
Architect for Schematic Design:
    Mithun
    Cearnal Andrulaitis
    (senior center, cottages and courtyard apartments)
Architect for Design Development:
    Mithun
    Cearnal Andrulaitis
    (senior center, cottages and courtyard apartments)
Interior Designer: Interspec
Landscape Designer: Arcadia Studio
Predominant Contractor:
    W.E. O'Neil Construction Co.
    Parton-Edwards Construction
    (senior center, cottages and courtyard apartments)

マラヴィラのねらい：
- サンタバーバラの高齢者が、上質でリラックスした雰囲気での屋外のライフスライルを満喫できるような、ランドマークとしてのシニアハウジングを創ること。
- この地方の伝統的なスパニッシュコロニアル・スタイルとの連続的な調和と、そのシニアリビングへの最適な適用。

Maravilla was conceived to:
- Create a landmark senior housing community that responds to local seniors' strong affinity for Santa Barbara's upscale, relaxed and outdoor lifestyle.
- Integrate seamlessly with the region's classic Spanish colonial vernacular, and at the same time be optimized for senior living.

自然との一体感がある健常棟のロビー前の庭
（写真：アーキテクチュラル・フォトグラフィ・インク）
Independent Living Courtyard off Lobby (photo: www.architecturephotoinc.com)

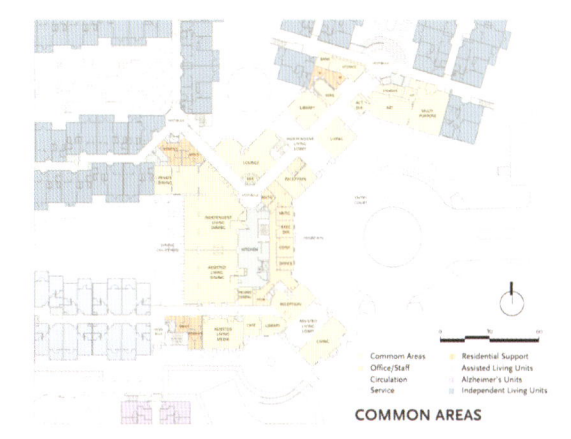

共用部平面図
Common area plan

Location: Santa Barbara, CA USA
Completion: 2004
Site Area: 81,000 sqm
Gross Floor Area: 35,100 sqm
Height: Under ground 1 story; Above ground 3 stories
Structure: Concrete structure
Number of Rooms: 363 rooms
Parking: 387 cars
Finishes:
<Predominant Exterior Wall>
    Stucco with Santa Barbara Finish
<Main lobby>
    Floor: Tile
    Wall: Paint
    Ceiling: Stained Wood
Award: Exhibition/Publication, Design for Aging Review 8, American Institute of Architects (AIA), 2005; Grand Award in Seniors' Housing-Gold Nugget Awards, Pacific Coast Builders Association, 2005; Platinum Winner, National Association of Home Builders (NAHB) Best of Seniors' Housing Design Awards, 2005; Project of the Year-Senior, Multifamily Executive Magazine, 2004; Award of Merit, American Planning Association, Central Coast Section, 2002

居室（写真：アーキテクチュラル・フォトグラフィ・インク）
Typical Residential Apartment (photo: www.architecturephotoinc.com)

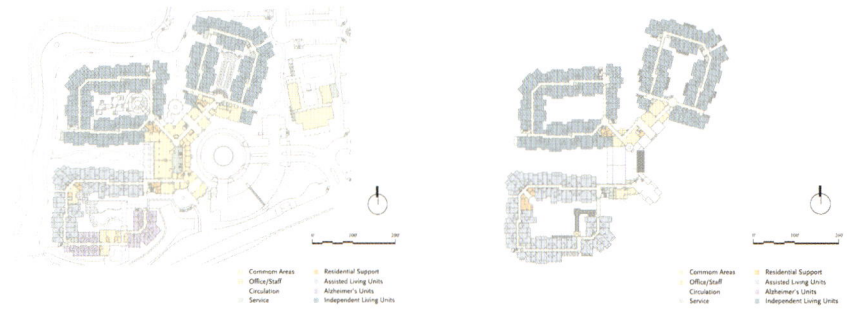

1階平面図
1st floor plan

2階平面図
2nd floor plan

81,000平方メートルの敷地規模にもかかわらず、マラヴィラの空間構成は明瞭である。ここではランドスケープの施された中庭や屋内の共用部の方へと向いているギャラリーやロッジアが動線となっており、居住者はそれらを楽しみながら住戸と共用部を行き来する。

Despite its 20-acre size, Maravilla is built around an organizing principle that makes it easy and intuitive to navigate. Circulation spaces are galleries and loggias that orient to vistas of the landscaped outdoor courtyards and indoor common spaces. Giving these spaces interior and exterior views helps residents make the passage from apartment to common areas more stimulating.

介護棟のロビー（写真：アーキテクチュラル・フォトグラフィ・インク）
Assisted Living Lobby (photo: www.architecturephotoinc.com)

Sun City Park Yokohama

サンシティパーク横浜

港町「横浜」を望む広大な丘陵地に創られた「公園のヴィレッジ」
"Villages on the park" with view to the lake and meadow, and Yokohama's harbor.

イースト・ヴィレッジの入り口（写真：ナカサ＆パートナーズ）
East Village Entry (photo: Nacasa & Partners)

ハーフ・センチュリー・モアによる約54,000平方メートルのこの施設は、横浜近郊の緑に恵まれた丘陵地に展開する。

施設全体は2つのヴィレッジからなるキャンパスを構成している。2つのヴィレッジを結ぶために設けられた南北に走る道沿いには、小川や木々、芝生のある中央庭園がある。この庭園によってキャンパスに統一感が与えられ、さらに周囲の自然との連続性が保たれている。

それぞれのヴィレッジには合計480室の健常者住戸が配されており、さらにウェスト・ビレッジには120室の介護用居室がある。小気味よいスケール感や仕上げに配慮しながら、建物を雁行させることで日差しや眺望に恵まれた良好な居住環境が確保されている。

2つのヴィレッジの共用部にはフォーマル・ダイニングやカジュアル・ダイニング、サンシィ・ホール、スパ・プール。コンサバトリー、ビリヤード・パーラーなどがある。小川には2つのヴィレッジを結ぶ橋が架けられており、そこでは居住者等が散策や景観を楽しむことができる。

中庭から見るイースト・ヴィレッジとウェスト・ヴィレッジを結ぶブリッジ（写真：ナカサ＆パートナーズ）
Exterior bridge from courtyard (photo: Naćasa & Partners)

Client: Half Century More Co., Ltd.
Master Designer: Perkins Eastman, Backen Arrigoni & Ross, Inc.
Architect for Schematic Design: Perkins Eastman, Kanko Kikaku Sekkeisha
Architect for Design Development: Perkins Eastman, Kanko Kikaku Sekkeisha
Interior Designer: Hirsch Bedner Associates
Landscape Designer: SWA Group
Predominant Contractor: Taisei Corporation

イースト・ヴィレッジのプール
（写真：ナカサ＆パートナーズ）
East Village Pool (photo: Naćasa & Partners)

木の素材を活かしたイースト・ヴィレッジのフォーマル・ダイニング
（写真：ナカサ＆パートナーズ）
East Village Formal Dining Room (photo: Naćasa & Partners)

In the midst of Yokohama's industrial bustle, Half Century More acquired 19 acres of rolling hillsides and mature forest for the new Sun City Park continuing care retirement community.

The 576,000 sf facility follows a one-campus, two-village plan. A new road meanders north to south through the site to connect two villages that bracket a central garden courtyard featuring a stream, mature gingkos, and rolling lawn. The park concept unfolds in a series of spaces, from a central garden that unifies the campus and creates a single identity for it, to the village gardens that open onto the forest and meadow.

Four hundred and eighty (480) independent living apartments are divided evenly between the East and West Villages, with a 120-room skilled nursing/dementia care facility integrated into the West Village. While Sun City Park Yokohama is a large facility overall in area and number of resident rooms, the client placed a high priority on responding to the scale of the individual resident. Large wings are stepped in plan to yield smaller neighborhoods, south-facing units maximize light quality and views, and both interior and exterior building materials blend into this unique setting.

Formal and casual dining rooms, as well as a full complement of public spaces, are available in both villages while campus-serving amenities like Sun City Hall, the spa and pool, the conservatory, and the billiards parlor are sprinkled between villages to encourage mixing. With the two villages connected by an enclosed bridge across the stream, residents enjoy a dramatic and welcoming experience while traversing from one building to another.

イースト・ヴィレッジのフォーマル・ダイニング入り口（写真：ナカサ＆パートナーズ）
East Village Formal Dining Room Entry (photo: Naćasa & Partners)

ウェスト・ヴィレッジのコンサバトリー（写真：ナカサ＆パートナーズ）
West Village Conservatory (photo: Naćasa & Partners)

水の流れのあるイースト・ヴィレッジのセントラルコート（写真：ナカサ＆パートナーズ）
East Village Central Court (photo: Naćasa & Partners)

雁行したファサード（写真：ナカサ＆パートナーズ）
West Village East Facade (photo: Naćasa & Partners)

窓辺にベンチがあるケアセンターのレジデントナーシング居室（写真：ナカサ＆パートナーズ）
Care Center Resident Nursing Room (photo: Naćasa & Partners)

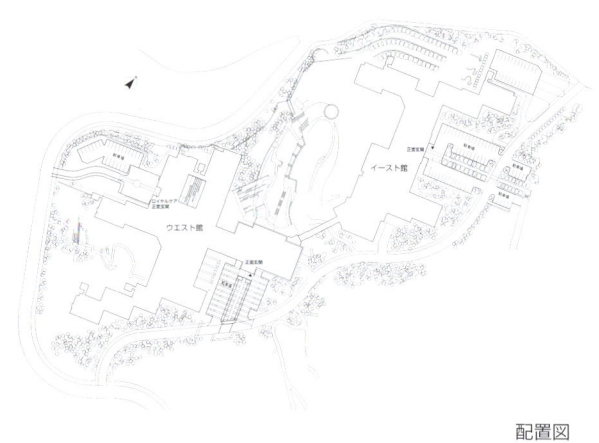

配置図
Site plan

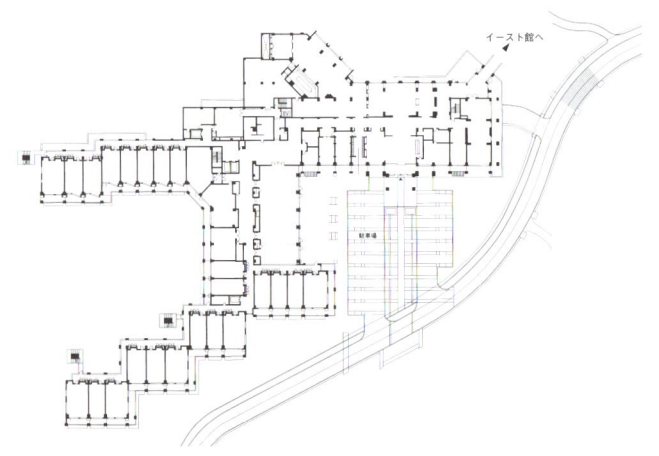

ウェスト・ヴィレッジ1階平面図
West Village 1st floor plan

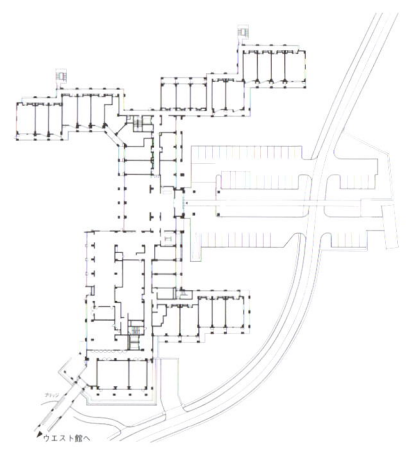

イースト・ヴィレッジ1階平面図
East Village 1st floor plan

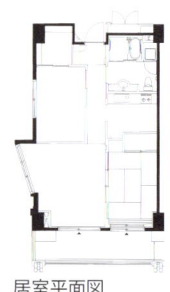

居室平面図
Unit plan

ウェスト・ヴィレッジのサロン（写真：ナカサ＆パートナーズ）
West Village Salon (photo: Naćasa & Partners)

Location: Yokohama, Kanagawa Japan
Completion: 2005
Site Area: 77,000 sqm
Gross Floor Area: 54,000 sqm
Height: Under ground 1 story; Above ground 6 stories
Structure: Concrete structure
Number of Rooms: 600 rooms
Parking: 155 cars
Finishes:
<Predominant Exterior Wall>
    Tile with Aluminum Trim
<Main lobby>
    Floor: Various Stone Tile
    Wall: Various Paneling:
        Wood Veneer, Vinyl Wall Covering, Stone Veneer
    Ceiling: Gypsum Board with Vinyl Wall Covering and Wood Trim

ケアセンターの自立生活ユニット（写真：ナカサ＆パートナーズ）
Care Center Independent Living Unit (photo: Naćasa & Partners)

Carlsbad by the Sea

カールスバッド・バイ・ザ・シー

南カリフォルニアのオーシャンビューと地域の伝統を活かしたCCRC
Multiple choices in living with spectacular ocean views in a quaint historic village.

太平洋へと延びる中庭の風景（写真：ティモシー・ヒューズレイ）
View of courtyard towards the ocean (photo: Timothy Hursley)

初期のカリフォルニア・ミッションリバイバル建築を偲ばせるカールスバッド・バイ・ザ・シー高齢者コミュニティは、その貴重な歴史的背景に敬意を表している。この建築制限の厳しい地域で、高齢者特有のニーズに応えながら過去への礼賛を示すことが、設計における課題であった。また、入居者が「その場所で年を重ねることができる」こと、を実現するために管理者が用意したプログラムは複雑なものであった。その他に安全性や建物のボリューム、スケール、高齢者にとって望ましい色彩なども慎重に検討された。

平均年齢が80歳という高齢者に伴う特殊な建築要件もあった。包括的なプログラムには、安全に関するものや公道を挟んでのアクセス、4.5メートルの敷地の高低差などに関するものが含まれていた。間接光や高齢者にとってわかりやすい色彩、手摺、テクスチュア、家具などが、建築デザインと違和感なく使われている。全般的に建物のデザインからは、「医療施設」ではなく「家」のような雰囲気が感じられる。

太平洋に面する敷地には、街の安全に関する規則や州の条例、港湾局や自治体による多くの制約があった。建物の高さやボリュームがさまざまであるのは、この敷地が3つの用途地域にまたがっているからでもある。さらに、施設設置基準に適合する養護施設は、単身者世帯の独立性を保ちながら、OSHPD ("Office of Statewide Health Planning and Development" in California = カリフォルニア州の医療施設の設置基準) に適合するように設計されている。

上にバルコニーのある介護施設の廊下（写真：ティモシー・ヒューズレイ）
Skilled nursing facility hallway (photo: Timothy Hursley)

Paying homage to its rich historical background, the Carlsbad by the Sea retirement community is reminiscent of early California mission revival architecture. Celebrating this past, while balancing the specialized needs of seniors within extremely stringent zoning and community limitations, provided challenging design obstacles. Further complicating the program was the desire of administrators to offer a full range of services that would allow residents the opportunity to "age in place". Design balance was achieved through emphasis on security, attention to massing and scale and use of color favorable to seniors.

Because the average age of residents is 80 years old, specific design requirements were needed. A comprehensive program addressed issues of security, accessibility divided by public streets and a grade differential varying fourteen feet from one end of the site to the other. Additionally, indirect lighting, and colors which were sympathetic to older persons' perception, handrails, textures and furniture were all integrated architecturally yet remain unobtrusive. Throughout the facility, residential scale and design elements were selected to create a home-like atmosphere rather than an institutional or hospital feel.

The project's location directly on the Pacific Ocean and within an active beach town community presented tremendous security issues and input from state-wide regulatory and coastal commission authorities and local city officials. Governed by three different zoning districts the site is subject to varying height and massing requirements. Additionally, the skilled nursing facility is designed in strict conformance with OSHPD standards, requiring a delicate balance between necessary hospital standards within finely grained single family neighborhood.

太平洋を望む屋上のパテイオ（写真：ティモシー・ヒューズレイ）
View on rooftop outdoor patio (photo: Timothy Hursley)

Client: Front Porch
Architect: Steinberg Architects
       Principal-In-Charge: David Mitani, AIA
       Design Principal: Robert Steinberg, FAIA
       Project Manager: Gladys Maldonado, AIA
Interior Designer: Robinson, Mills + Williams
Landscape Designer: The SWA Group
Predominant Contractor: DPR Construction, Inc.

海側の外観（写真：ティモシー・ヒューズレイ）
View of beachfront (photo: Timothy Hursley)

「このプロジェクトは、複雑な敷地がかかえる多くの物理的・法的制限にもかかわらず、多くの点で成功している。我々は絶景のオーシャンビューを活かしながら、プロジェクトをこの洒落た歴史的な街と調和させた。しかしカールスバッドの最大の特徴は、居住者の自立性を促進しながら選択性の幅を広げていることや、カリフォルニアスタイルのさまざまな中庭を配したレイアウトである。」

スタインバーグ・アーキテクツ
プリンシパル
デイビッド・ミタニ、米国建築家協会会員

"Although this was a very complicated site with many physical and approval constraints, the project succeeds on many levels. We were able to take advantage of the spectacular ocean views and integrate the project with the historic village. What's really great about Carlsbad by the Sea, though, is the layout. It promotes independence with multiple choices in living accommodations and integrates classic California courtyards."

David Mitani, AIA
Principal
Steinberg Architects

ロビーと受付（写真：ティモシー・ヒューズレイ）
Lobby reception (photo: Timothy Hursley)

Location: Carlsbad, CA U.S.A.
Completion: 1998
Site Area: 9,400 sqm
Gross Floor Area: 25,700 sqm
Height: Under ground 1 story; Above ground 3 stories
Structure: Steel and Concrete structure
Number of Rooms: 207 rooms
        160 independent living units
        14 assisted living units
        33 skilled-nursing beds
Parking: 274 cars
<Predominant Exterior Wall>
        Plaster
<Main lobby>
        Floor: Tile
        Wall: Wood
        Ceiling: Wood
Award:
1999 Gold Award, NAHB Best of Senior Housing Awards, Continuing Care Retirement Community
1999 Grand Award, Pacific Coast Builders Conference/Builder Magazine, Assisted Living Community
1999 Design For Aging: 2000 Review, Exhibition and Publication, American Institute of Architects
1999 Grand Award, Pacific Coast Builders Conference/BuilderMagazine, Best Mixed Use Project

一般住宅のスケール感の道路側の側面（写真：ティモシー・ヒューズレイ）
View along side road (photo: Timothy Hursley)

介護居室（写真：ティモシー・ヒューズレイ）
Skilled nursing facility bedroom (photo: Timothy Hursley)

介護施設のロビー（写真：ティモシー・ヒューズレイ）
Skilled nursing facility lobby (photo: Timothy Hursley)

配置図
Site plan

4階平面図
4th floor plan

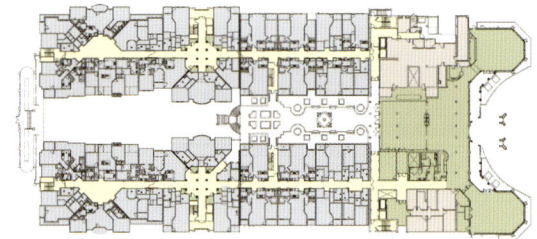

2階平面図
2nd floor plan

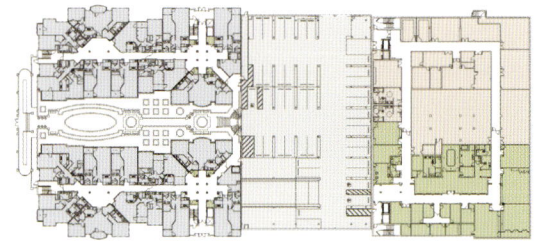

1階平面図
1st floor plan

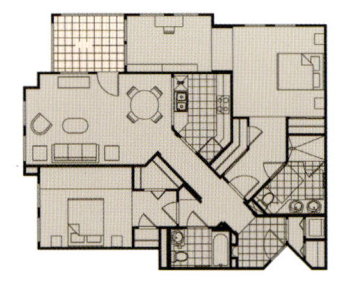

プレミアム・ツーベッドルーム平面図
Premium two bedroom plan

中庭から入り口方向を見る（写真：ティモシー・ヒューズレイ）
Courtyard view inward (photo: Timothy Hursley)

スパ・プール（写真：ティモシー・ヒューズレイ）
Spa pool (photo: Timothy Hursley)

ナースステーション（写真：ティモシー・ヒューズレイ）
Skilled nursing facility nurse station (photo: Timothy Hursley)

Diage Kobe
ディアージュ神戸

高級感あふれる空間で自由に快適に暮らすリタイヤメントの住まい
A luxury residence for retirements with sense of freedom and comfort.

ディアージュ神戸を中心に、周辺環境を空撮（平成16年9月撮影）
Aerial view with surrounding environment of the Diage Koge (dated September 2004)

異国情緒あふれる神戸の中心三宮からJR快速で約17分垂水駅の北約6kmの閑静な住宅街のすぐ隣に堂々と佇むディアージュ神戸は三菱グループの総力を結集し創り上げた介護付有料老人ホームである。約4,900坪の敷地に、健常者が利用する地上14階建ての住宅棟（175戸）と、要介護者が利用する地上5階地下1階建ての介護棟（100室）からなっている。

住宅棟は高級感のある建物造りをテーマとし、ホテルのような空間作りを目指した。外光をふんだんに取り入れた人工大理石床のエントランスロビーからは風景画のような山並みが眺められる。1階にある男女大浴場は加温循環式の天然温泉と清水の2浴槽からなり、温泉効果が期待でき、この他にもライブラリーや創作工房、シアタールーム、カラオケルーム等を備えた共用施設が充実している。2階には瀬戸内海を一望し、神戸の夜景が望めるメインダイニングがあり、3食とも予約なしのフルサービスとなっている。また家族や友達同士の食事会には、プライベートダイニングで特別メニューを楽しむことが出来る。

住戸最大の特徴はバリアフリーは当然のこととし、廊下は車椅子対応の幅を確保するなど高齢者対応の設計を取り入れながらも、あくまで普通の住まいであることをコンセプトにしている点にある。各戸には24時間対応の生活リズムセンサーやナースコール、モニター付玄関インターホンなどを装備し、緊急時や日常の安全面に配慮している。また住まいを基本とする考え方から、リビングには床暖房を設置、食器洗い乾燥機付システムキッチンやノンタッチ便座、一般住宅用より一回り大きなバスタブを設置したカラリ床の浴室もあり、プライバシーを守ると共に便利で安心快適な生活空間を提供している。

西側隣接の垂水ゴルフ倶楽部より見る住宅棟外観。全戸南向きで眺める景色は見る人の心を穏やかにする。
Exterior view of residential tower from the Tarumi Golf Club on the west. View from all of residential units facing south makes residents comfortable.

The Diage Kobe, a CCRC developed through whole expertise of the Mitsubishi group, is located adjacent to gentle residential area, 6 km away from the Tarumi rail station, 17 minutes express train ride from Sannomiya, center of Kobe with an exotic mood, to north. On the land of 16,200 sqm, facility consists of a residential tower with 14 stories housing 175 independent living units and a care center with 1 under ground and 5 stories housing 100 care units.

Residential tower, aiming at luxurious facility, is designed to create environment of hotels. Entrance lobby filled with natural sun light and finished with marble stone on the floor views spectacular scenery of mountains. Public facility include large bath rooms on the 1st floor for men/women with two bath tubs incorporating natural hot spring with heated circulation and pure water for the effect of hot spring, library, craft room, theatre room, Karaoke room and others. Main dining on the 2nd floor viewing Setonaikai and night scenery of Kobe serves breakfast, lunch and dinner without reservation. And private dining serves family or friends with special menu.

Featuring point of the design concept was to create a Home with ideas of responding to life of senior citizens...barrier free, wide corridor for wheelchair use. For securing resident from emergency, 24 hours life-rhythm sensor, nurse call, interphone with monitor and others are installed. And aiming to life at the Home with convenience, safety and comfort, floor heating in living room, wash/dray machine in kitchen, non-touch device in toilet, and larger tub and dry floor in bath room are prepared.

神戸ならではのパノラマを望むスカイガーデン
The sky garden providing a beautiful panoramic view of Kobe

Client: Kinki Ryoju Estate Co., Ltd.
Master Designer: Yamasita Sekkei, Ink. Kansai Branch
Architect for Schematic Design: Yamasita Sekkei, Ink. Kansai Branch
Architect for Design Development: Yamasita Sekkei, Ink. Kansai Branch
Predominant Contractor: Obayashi Corporation

雨の日でもぬれずに車から乗り降りできる大庇のあるエントランス車寄せ
Residents drop off from car at the porte-cochere with a large canopy, without wet in rainy day.

日常的に介護が必要な方が入居する介護棟。
住宅棟からの住み替えも可能。
Care center for residents requiring care...
available relocation from the residential tower

本施設の設計及び運営の根底にあるのは介護先進国スウェーデンの「高齢者医療・福祉の三原則」である。
1) 自己決定の尊重
　・「施設」ではなく「住宅」で自分らしく
　・サービスメニューを豊富に準備し、それを選択できるだけの環境（建築・設備）を整える
2) 継続性の重視
　・介護度の進行を想定した（簡単な改修で使い続けられる）住まいづくり
　・一時介護室（体調不良、退院直後など健康不安がある場合のケアルーム）の活用
3) 残存能力・潜在能力の活用
　・園芸療法（施設全体で6箇所の庭園を設置）への取り組み、等
上記を具現化すべく、国内外のさまざまな施設を見学し議論を重ねてきた。ハードおよびソフトの両面での更なる進化をめざして検討・努力中である。

Basic idea of design and operation of this facility is the "three principal of medical care/welfare for senior citizen" of Sweden, front runner of elderly care that is:
1) respect on self decision
　・Self identity not in "Institution" but in "Home"
　・Preparation of variety of service menu and environment (architecture/MEP) for choice by residents
2) importance of continuity
　・Creation of home acceptable progress of level of care (usable with light modification)
　・Application of temporal care unit (care room in case of bad health or uneasiness of condition immediate after leaving)
3) application of remaining abilities and potential capacities
　・Application of garden therapy (there are six gardens in the site.), and others

To attain ideas above, we visited various facilities, nation wide and overseas, and discussed over and over again.
Now believing that we provide the facility with sophisticated hardware and operation, still we seek evolution for better services.

美しい夜景を楽しみながら食事を楽しめるメインダイニング
Main dining to experience the best of the time - serving delicious foods with view of beautiful night scenery

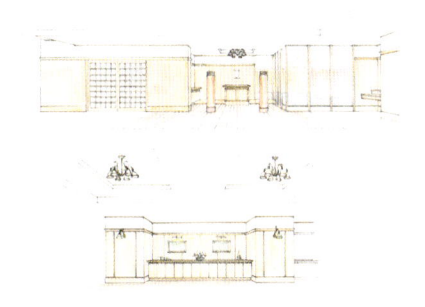

エントランスロビーのスケッチ
Sketch of entrance lobby

映画や音楽鑑賞には最適な設備のシアタールーム
Theatre room equiped with tecnology for movie and music

Location: Kobe-shi, Hyogo Japan
Completion: 2004
Site Area: 16,223 sqm
Gross Floor Area: 29,711 sqm
Height: Under ground 1 story; Above ground 14 stories
Structure: Steel and Reinforced Concrete structure
Number of Rooms: 275 rooms
　　　　　　　　(independent 175/nursing unit 100)
Parking: 48 cars
Finishes:
<Predominant Exterior Wall>
　　　Ceramic Tile
<Main lobby>
　　　Floor: Marble Stone with Carpet
　　　Wall: Wood
　　　Ceiling: EP

大理石張りの床が広がる格調高いインテリアのエントランスロビー
Entrance lobby with luxurious interior with marble stone on the floor

ダイニングを取り囲む介護居室の配置（クラスター型ユニット）は、家族的な雰囲気の中で生活を楽しむことができる。
Unita on the 1st floor in the care center: clustered rooms are distributed around dining area

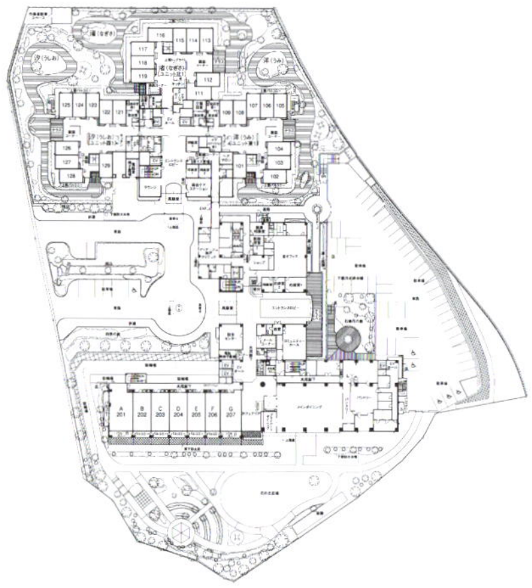

配置図
Site plan

住宅棟居室
Residnets room in residential tower

居室平面図
Unit plan

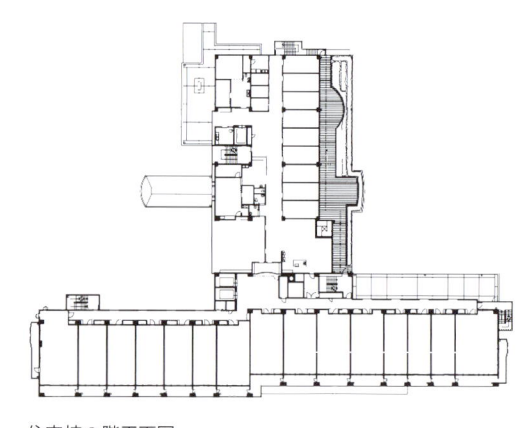

住宅棟 2 階平面図
2nd floor plan of residential tower

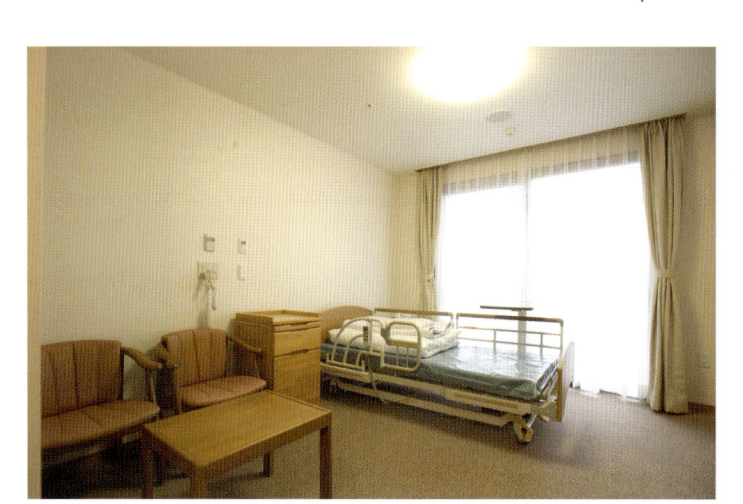

急な発熱や退院後の不安な時期に利用する一時介護室
Temporal care room for immediate fever or uneasy period after leaving the facility

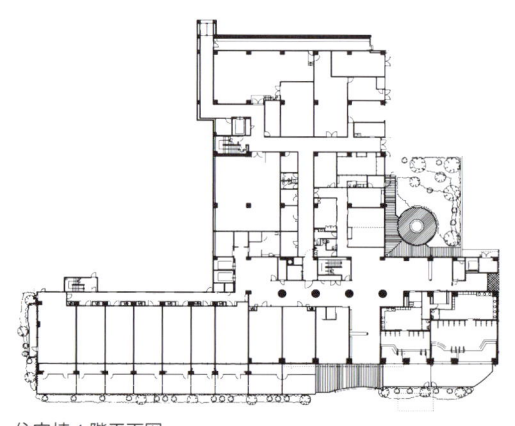

住宅棟 1 階平面図
1st floor plan of residential tower

118　ディアージュ神戸

介護棟居室
Care unit

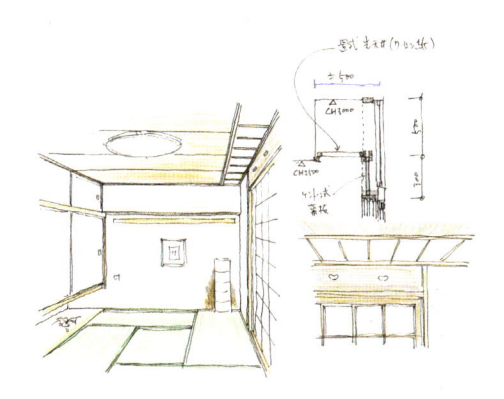

和室の詳細なスケッチ
Sketch of detail in Japanese style room

離宮庵：石楠花の庭に面した和室は、いけばな、書道、会合などに使用される。
The Rikyuan: Japanese style room, facing to rosebay garden, for flower arranging, writing, and meeting

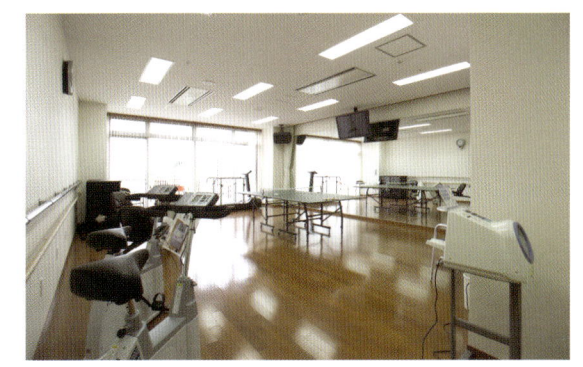

大浴場「やすらぎ」：癒しの天然温泉（加温・循環ろ過）。含弱放射能、ナトリウム、炭酸水素塩、塩化物温泉
A large public bath "Yasuragi": natural hot spring for healing (additional heat/circulated filtering) with light radioactivity, sodium, carbon hydrochloric acid, and chloride.

フィットネスでは筋力トレーニングで体力の維持や増進をはかる
Fitness room for physical exercise to maintain healthy condition

大浴場
Communal bathing

Twin Lakes at Montgomery
ツインレークス・モンゴメリー

都市に隣接する街に組み込まれた終身介護型キャンパス
CCRC campus integrated into a small town urban area directly adjacent to downtown.

健常棟の外観（写真：ジェイソン・メイヤー、フェインノフ・フォトグラフィ）
Exterior rear view of independent living apartments (photo: Jason Meyer of Feinknopf Photography)

この斬新な終身介護型のキャンパスは、オハイオ州モンゴメリー市の中心部に近いこの街によく調和している。居住者は施設内のサービスやアメニティを楽しむだけでなく、より大きなコミュニティである街の銀行や薬局、映画館、レストランなどに気軽にでかけることができる。さらにツインレークスは、この高齢者コミュニティとモンゴメリーの住人や若者達との交流を促進する施設でもある。

2つの印象的な2層のロトンダの周りに、この施設は構成されている。居住者が、先進的なウェルネスセンターやメイン・ダイニングルームなどに気軽に行けるように、サービスとアメニティはロトンダの付近に配されている。93戸のアパートと125戸のコテージ、27室の介護居室、16床の特別介護ベッド、20床のナーシングベッドがある。エデンの哲学に基づいて創られた特別介護・認知症棟では、居住者の要望に対応しながら、動植物のある環境で自宅にいるような感覚で生活を送ることができる。

タウンスクエア（写真：ジェイソン・メイヤー、フェインノフ・フォトグラフィ）
Town square (photo: Jason Meyer of Feinknopf Photography)

The design for this exceptional new CCRC focuses on integrating the facility's campus into a small town urban area located directly adjacent to the downtown area of Montgomery, Ohio. Residents enjoy not only services and amenities within the facility, but they also have ease of access to this quaint small town's local bank, pharmacy, movie theatre, restaurants and more - making them a true part of the larger community. There is also an intergenerational component to Twin Lakes, further linking the community to the residents and connecting them to the youngest generation of Montgomery. The facility's design revolves around the creation of two impressive, two-story rotundas. Services and amenities are located off each of the rotundas giving residents quick and easy access to the places they need to go, such as the state-of-the-art wellness center and the formal dining room. It also contains 93 apartments, 125 cottages, 27 assisted living apartments, 16 special care beds, and 20 nursing beds. Responding to resident needs, the special care/dementia wing incorporates the Eden philosophy of care, which allows residents to flourish in a more homelike, nurturing environment among plants and animals.

Client: Life Enriching Communities
Master Designer: FreemanWhite, Inc.
Architect for Schematic Design: FreemanWhite, Inc.
Architect for Design Development: FreemanWhite, Inc.
Interior Designer: FreemanWhite, Inc.
Predominant Contractor: Weitz

チャペル（写真：ジェイソン・メイヤー、フェインノフ・フォトグラフィ）
Chapel (photo: Jason Meyer of Feinknopf Photography)

プール（写真：ジェイソン・メイヤー、フェインノフ・フォトグラフィ）
Pool at wellness center (photo: Jason Meyer of Feinknopf Photography)

ジュースバー（写真：ジェイソン・メイヤー、フェインノフ・フォトグラフィ）
Juice bar (photo: Jason Meyer of Feinknopf Photography)

メイン・ダイニングルーム（写真：ジェイソン・メイヤー、フェインノフ・フォトグラフィ）
Formal dining room (photo: Jason Meyer of Feinknopf Photography)

共用棟の居間（写真：ジェイソン・メイヤー、フェインノフ・フォトグラフィ）
Living room in commons building (photo: Jason Meyer of Feinknopf Photography)

カフェダイニング（写真：ジェイソン・メイヤー、フェインノフ・フォトグラフィ）
Cafe dining (photo: Jason Meyer of Feinknopf Photography)

Twin Lakes at Montgomery 123

メモリーサポート・ユニットの居間（写真：ジェイソン・メイヤー、フェインノフ・フォトグラフィ）
Living room in memory support unit (photo: Jason Meyer of Feinknopf Photography)

住戸のダイニング（写真：ジェイソン・メイヤー、フェインノフ・フォトグラフィ）
Apart Dining (photo: Jason Meyer of Feinknopf Photography)

住戸の居間（写真：ジェイソン・メイヤー、フェインノフ・フォトグラフィ）
Apart Living (photo: Jason Meyer of Feinknopf Photography)

配置図
Site plan

2階平面図
2nd floor plan

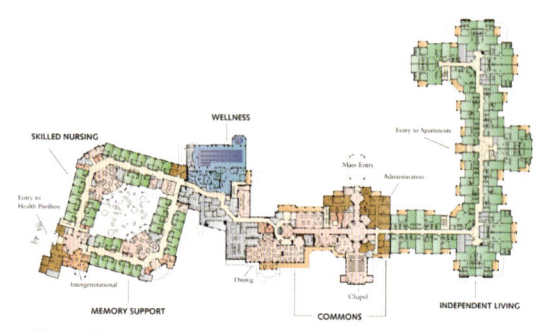

1階平面図
1st floor plan

Location: Cincinnati, Ohio U.S.A.
Completion: 2005
Site Area: 226,600 sqm
Gross Floor Area: 30,240 sqm
Height: 3 plus underground garage
Structure: Steel structure
Number of Rooms:
  125 cottages
  93 apartments
  27 assisted living apartments
  20 skilled nursing beds
  16 special care beds
Parking: 160 above ground, 50 under ground cars
Finishes:
<Predominant Exterior Wall>
  Brick with Composite Shingle Roof
<Main lobby>
  Floor: Carpet with Wood Accents
  Wall: Vinyl Wall Covering and Paint
  Ceiling: GWB / Acoustical Panels / Stretch PVC

ヘルス棟の玄関（写真：ジェイソン・メイヤー、フェインノフ・フォトグラフィ）
Entry to Health Pavilion (photo: Jason Meyer of Feinknopf Photography)

健常棟居室階のロビー（写真：ジェイソン・メイヤー、フェインノフ・フォトグラフィ）
Lobby space on independent living floor (photo: Jason Meyer of Feinknopf Photography)

Twin Lakes at Montgomery

Seniorenhaus St. Nikolaus
シニオレンハウス・セントニコラス

陽光に満ちた場、そして屋内外の環境が相互に貫入するファサード
A place in the sunshine, and mutual boundary between inside and outside.

南側のアプローチ（写真：マルゲリータ・スピルティニ）
Approach south (photo: Margherita Spiluttini)

ザルツブルグ地方の空間
瀟洒な家のような空間
55の個室が小さな街を創る

「屋内」
玄関前広場からセントニコラス高齢者施設に入ると人は光の中に立つ。そこでは、居住者とビジターとの静かな語らいの断片やエスプレッソバーからのコーヒーの香り、穏やかで清楚な建物の色彩が我々を包み込む。
そこは全てのことがその周りで展開するハブとして機能する、緑のオアシスである。
この空間は高齢者施設における機能の2つの側面をまかなっている。ここは、空間の面白さや快適性を損なうことなく、職員が作業を行う空間であると同時にビジターが行き先の方向を知ることができる通路である。
この内部空間は直線的に配された2つの居住棟に沿って構成されている。居室の入口脇にはベンチがあり、広場や緑豊かな屋外への眺望のあるニッチのある居室が小さな家のように並べられている。居室の色彩の使い分けは、自分の家である個室を認識するのに役立っている。
その空間の質の良さは感覚的にも空間的にも体験し得る。光とガラス、木材の使用によって、この地方の伝統と高齢者施設に対する現代的解釈が表現されている。ザルツブルグ地方でよく使用されている木材で創られた外壁は内部へと続いている。ガラスパネルを多用したファサードには流れるような連続性がある。ガラスの見晴台は、緑の中で腰掛けることのできる大きな「居間」である。そこでは屋外は屋内に転じ、屋内の居室は屋外へと延伸している。建物は環境に語りかけ、環境そのものとなる。

北側の住棟間（写真：マルゲリータ・スピルティニ）
In between north (photo: Margherita Spiluttini)

A room in the Salzburger Land.
A room like a small house.
55 rooms make a small town.

(Inside)
We enter the "St. Nikolaus" retirement home via the entrance court and stand in the light. Softly spoken snatches of residents' and visitors' conversation waft over to us, together with the scent of coffee from the espresso bar and the calm and serene colours of the building.

We are standing in the main hall, a green oasis that serves as the hub around which everything revolves.

This space serves to guarantee the double life a retirement home must lead: clear and short paths that guarantee functional and professional working conditions for staff and help visitors to orientate themselves whilst not denying either spatial variety or a comfortable atmosphere.

This space organises the interior along two linear residential streets. The rooms are lined up like small houses, with a bench before each entrance and each bench in a niche with a view either onto the square or towards the greenery outside. Colours that are assigned to each residential section help to locate each room, each house.

The evidence of high quality can be perceived emotionally and experienced both spatially and sensually: light, glass and timber combine tradition with a modern interpretation of a retirement home. The exterior skin made of timber, a tried and tested element typical of the Salzburg area, is continued inside. Facade and glass panelling build a continuous haptic unity.

Glass gazebos enlarge every "living room" with a sitting area in the greenery. Outside turns toward inside, inside presses outward - the building talks to the environment and becomes one itself.

Seniorenhaus St. Nikolaus

1階のラウンジ（写真：マルゲリータ・スピルティニ）
First floor lounge (photo: Margherita Spiluttini)

東側カフェのロッジア（写真：マルゲリータ・スピルティニ）
East cafe loggias (photo: Margherita Spiluttini)

Client: Gemeindeverband Neumarkt am Wallersee
Master Designer: Di Stefan Haass
Architect for Schematic Design: Di Stefan Haass
Architect for Design Development:
    Di Bernd Rickert
    Di Arnd Schule
    Di Frank Berners

1階のカフェ（写真：マルゲリータ・スピルティニ）
First floor cafe (photo: Margherita Spiluttini)

グランドフロアーの廊下（写真：マルゲリータ・スピルティニ）
Ground floor hallway (photo: Margherita Spiluttini)

Location: Salzburg Austria
Completion: 2001
Site Area: 4,616 sqm
Gross Floor Area: 3,912 sqm
Height: Under ground 1 story; Above ground 2 stories
Structure: Steel and Concrete, Wood structure
Number of Rooms: 56 rooms
Parking: 20 cars
Finishes:
<Predominant Exterior Wall>
    Wood and Glass
<Main lobby>
    Floor: Stone
    Wall: Gipskarton and Wood
    Ceiling: Gipskarton and Glass
Award: Architecture Award, Province of Salzburg, 2001

標準居室（写真：マルゲリータ・スピルティニ）
Room typical (photo: Margherita Spiluttini)

Seniorenhaus St. Nikolaus

スケッチ
Sketch

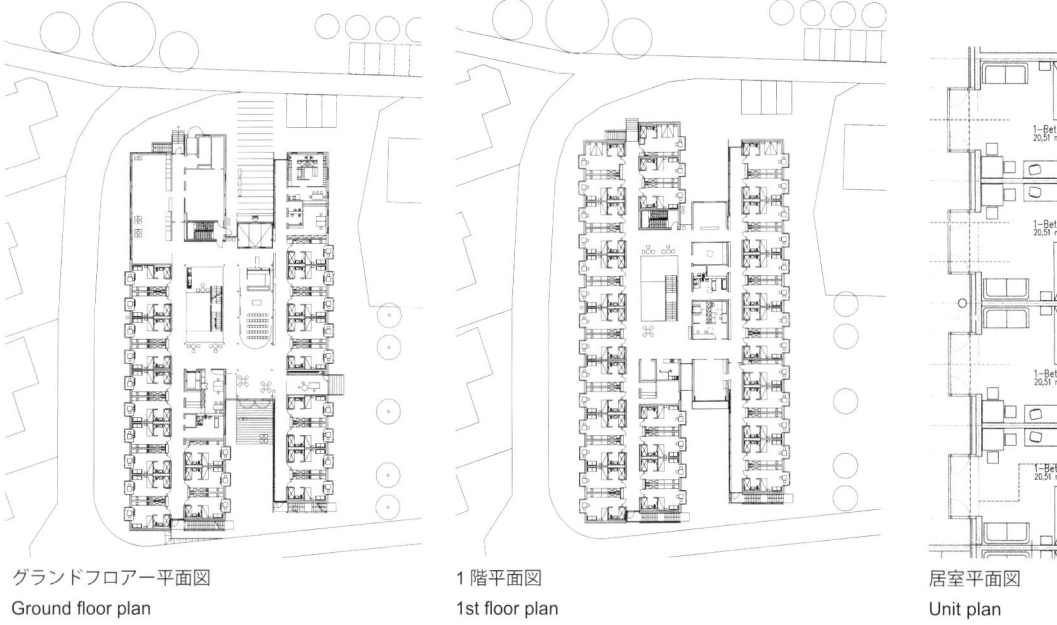

配置図
Site plan

グランドフロアー平面図
Ground floor plan

1階平面図
1st floor plan

居室平面図
Unit plan

「屋外」

屋内の構成の特徴は、この小規模な街におけるコンパクトな建物の外観としてもあらわれている。それは気さくな佇まいで存在している。それは独特であるが異質でない。周辺環境のスケールへの配慮から、建物は2階建とし、居室は並べて配されている。単身者棟のガラスの見晴台からは屋外を伺うことができる。密集した建物は周囲からの視線を遮る。屋内の緑のオアシスが延伸した屋外の庭を創るために、建物は意図的に小ぢんまりとさせている。自由に動き廻れる部分と管理された部分との境界は屋外にあり、セントニコラスの居住者が孤立感を感じないように配慮している。

ここでは、木で囲まれた建物の全体的な雰囲気を見晴台のガラスのところで崩しながら、建物の内部と外部の境界をまたいだ生活が営まれる。ガラスの開放性と木材の守護性とのコントラストは、中の高齢者の生活を反映している。それは外部のコミュニティと中での生活との関係を開いたり濾過する外皮ともいえる。セントニコラスは人工的環境における高齢者の生活のベンチマークといえる。55室の居室からなるこの小さな街は、今日も夕明りの中で映えている。

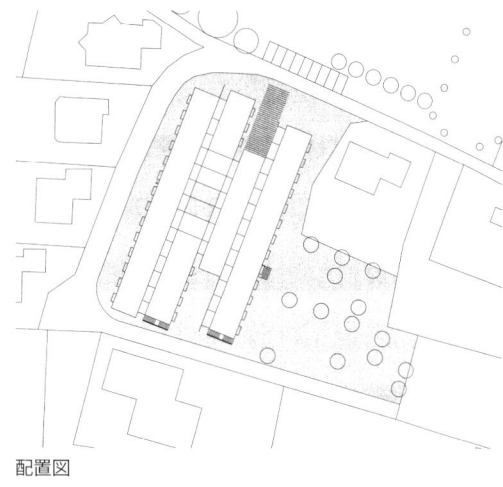

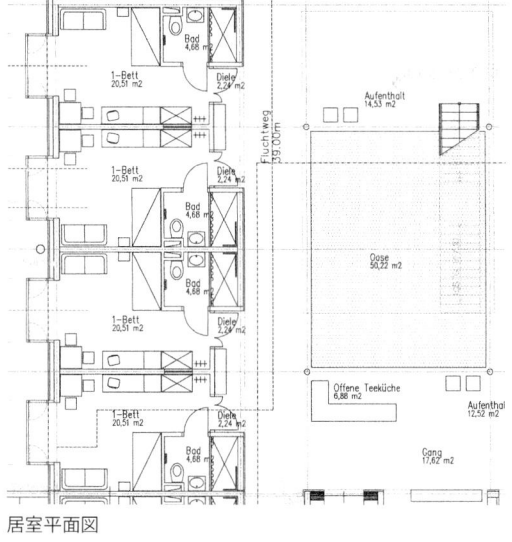

(Outside)

The focused organisation of the interior results in a compact building body in the small-scale urban context. It integrates without ingratiating. It looks different but not alien. The two-storey solution and arrangement of the residential rows respect the scale of the environment. The glass gazebos of the solitary building make the individual housing units visible to the outside. The house is dense, and it breaks clear. The built-up floor area is deliberately minimal, making space for a garden that continues the interior "green oasis" to the outside. The boundary between control and free space is part of the planning of the external space but does not convey to the inhabitants of "St. Nikolaus" any feeling of being isolated

The building draws life from crossing the limit between inside and outside, from continuity of timber bars, breaching the spatial skin in the area of the gazebos and the atmosphere created through the holistic use of the timber. The contrasts between glass and timber, openness and security, reflect the life of the elderly people in the building: the protecting skin, which consciously both opens and filters a connection with the community and life around the building. The life of the inhabitants of "St. Nikolaus" is the benchmark for the built space. We are leaving the building in the evening sunlight of late afternoon; 55 rooms make a small town.

南側の中庭（写真：マルゲリータ・スピルティニ）
Yard south (photo: Margherita Spiluttini)

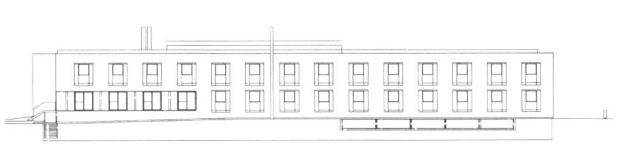

東立面図
East elevation

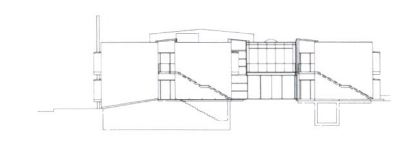

南立面図
South elevation

西立面図
West elevation

1階の廊下（写真：マルゲリータ・スピルティニ）
First floor yard hallway (photo: Margherita Spiluttini)

Seniorenhaus St. Nikolaus

The Atrium at Cedars Retirement Community

ザ・アトリウム・シダース・リタイアメントコミュニティ

アトリウムと3つのウィングを持つ、美しい庭園を囲んで展開する施設

Upscale Retirement Housing with three residential wings extending from a three-story sky lit atrium and landscaped courtyard.

スカイライトのあるアトリウムから延びる3つの居住部のウィングによる建物の構成は、住宅のスケール感をもったボリュームである。T型平面の北ウィングをオフセットすることで形成されたアトリウムは、荘厳な松林の景色へと開かれている。居住者が方向感覚を得られるように、アトリウムは建物の中心部に意図的に配されている。屋内の共用部の通路やギャラリーはアトリウムからの明りで照らされ、その明るさはガラスの間仕切りを通して部屋の中にまで及んでいる。

ランドスケープが施された庭が、隣接するナーシングセンターとの間にある。この施設は将来、介護施設や既存のナーシングセンターにある管理棟と連結される予定で、それによって職員や居住者は屋内通路を使って施設間を移動することができるようになる。敷地計画では、湿地の自然林を保全することに細心の注意がはらわれた。

自然光に恵まれた、繊細なディテールやエレガントなプロポーションのアトリウムは、快適な居住性と精神性の確保に資している。屋内通路やギャラリーなどの空間は、アトリウムからの採光やガラスの間仕切りによって明るさで満たされている。見通しの良いグランドフロアでは、ビジターは奥へと導かれる。表玄関のロビーがランドスケープの施された庭との軸線上に配されている。ロビーの中央ではカフェの湾曲したガラスが、アトリウムのある右側へと視線を導く。アトリウムからはアーチのあるギャラリーや会議室、メイン・ダイニングルームが続く。

アトリウム正面（写真：ボンジュール・スタジオズ）
Atrium Front (photo: Bonjour Studios)

3階から見る3層の吹き抜け（写真：ボンジュール・スタジオズ）
Three Story Atrium from 3rd Floor (photo: Bonjour Studios)

Client: Jewish Home for Aged; Kathryn Callnan, CEO
Architect: Tsomides Associates Architects Planners/TAAP
Master Designer: Constantine L. Tsomides, NCARB, AIA
MArch, Columbia Univ; MDesS, Harvard GSD
Design Team: Thomas J. McBride, Jerald W. Durr, Scott C. Roberts,
Diana G. Tsomides, Anne-Marie Vawter
Interior Designer: Currier & Associates
Landscape Designer: Land Use Consultants
Predominant Contractor: C. M. Cimino, Inc.

The facility was designed with three residential wings extending from a three-story sky lit atrium to create residential scaled building masses. The atrium, formed by offsetting the north wing of the T-shaped plan, was oriented toward views of majestic pine trees to the north. It was strategically located at the core of the building to aid residents' orientation. Internal public circulation spaces and gallery areas are infused with daylight from the atrium and receive borrowed light through glazed interior partitions.

The building shape combined with the adjacent nursing center forms a landscaped courtyard. The facility will connect in the future to an Assisted Living Facility, currently being designed, and the Administration wing of the existing Nursing Center, providing direct enclosed access between facilities for staff and residents. Great care was taken to reserve the natural wooded site with the wetlands.

The intimately detailed and elegantly proportioned Atrium space, bathed in natural light, enhances the living experience and stimulates mental alertness. Internal public circulation spaces and gallery areas are infused with daylight through glazed borrowed-light interior partitions along the common support spaces and from the Atrium, which spatially explodes outward and upward. The Ground Floor Plan leads the visitor through a sequence of spaces, drawn forward by vistas beyond. The Main Entry Lobby lies directly on axis with the landscaped rear courtyard. At the Lobby midpoint, the curved glazed partition of the Cafe guides one's eyes to the right, toward the three-story Atrium beyond. From the Atrium, one is drawn to the arched Gallery, leading to the Meeting Rooms and main Dining Room.

ダイニングルームへと続くギャラリー（写真：ボンジュール・スタジオズ）
Arched Gallery leading to Dining (photo: Bonjour Studios)

表玄関のロビーとカフェ（写真：ボンジュール・スタジオズ）
Main Entry Lobby & Cafe (photo: Bonjour Studios)

プール棟のあるランドスケープの施された中庭（写真：ボンジュール・スタジオズ）
Landscaped Courtyard with Pool Pavilion (photo: Bonjour Studios)

マスタープランのスタディ模型（左に既存のナーシングセンター、中央に将来の介護棟、右に既存のアトリウム・アト・シダース）（写真：コンスタンティン・トミデス）
Master Plan Study Model (Exist. Nursing Ctr at left, Prop. ALF at center, Exist."The Atrium at Cedars" at right.) (photo: Constantine Tsomides)

3層のアトリウムに隣接するエレベータ・ロビーを中心に配されている居室階は、ガラスの間仕切りによってやわらかく区画されている。基準階の平面をT型とすることで、厨房やダイニングへの採光や、各階に8つの理想的なコーナーユニットの設置が可能となった。

The typical residential floor has a centrally located Elevator Lobby adjacent to the three-story Atrium courtyard, yet discreetly screened by a glazed partition. The modified T shape of the typical floor plan provides eight desirable corner units per floor, making it possible to install windows to the Kitchens and Dining Areas.

アトリム背面（写真：ボンジュール・スタジオズ）
Atrium Rear (photo: Bonjour Studios)

左側に将来の介護棟があるレンダリング（レンダリング：トッドキャド）
Rendering Showing Future ALF on left (Rendering: TodoCad)

表玄関（写真：ボンジュール・スタジオズ）
Main Entrance (photo: Bonjour Studios)

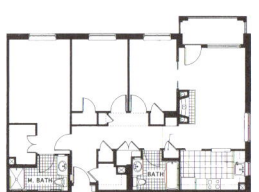

ツーベッド ルーム・デラックス
平面図
Two Bedroom Deluxe

住戸（写真：ボンジュール・スタジオズ）
Residents room (photo: Bonjour Studios)

1階平面図
1st floor palan

Location: Portland, ME U.S.A.
Completion: 2000
Site Area: 40,460 sqm
Gross Floor Area: 9,750 sqm
Height: Under ground 1 story; Aabove ground 3 stories
Structure: Steel and Concrete structure
Number of Rooms: 61 Apartments /rooms
Parking: 65 cars
Finishes:
<Predominant Exterior Wall>
    Brick and Precast Concrete
<Main lobby>
    Floor: Carpet
    Wall: Wall Covering and Paint
    Ceiling: Acoustic Tile and Drywall
Award: The Best of Seniors' Housing Gold Award, National Association of Home Builders, National Council on Seniors' Housing, 2001; Design 2002 Magazine, Featured New Construction Projects in Long Term Care, 2002; America Institute of Architect/American Association of Homes and Services for the Aging, Design for Aging Review 6th Edition, Featured Project, 2004.
Publication: Featured on cover of Urban Land Institute book, "Analyzing Seniors' Housing Markets," by Susan B. Brecht, ULI 2002

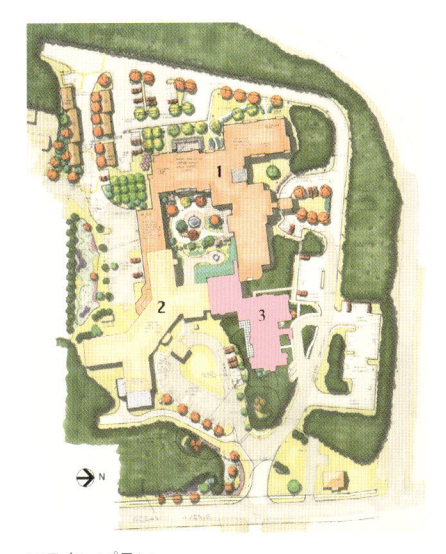

マスタープラン
Master Plan

断面図
Section

3階（写真：ボンジュール・スタジオズ）
Third Floor (photo: Bonjour Studios)

セラピーラッププール（写真：ボンジュール・スタジオズ）
Therapy Lap Pool (photo: Bonjour Studios)

左にライブラリーのあるカフェ（写真：ボンジュール・スタジオズ）
Cafe with Library at left (photo: Bonjour Studios)

The Atrium at Cedars Retirement Community

Sun City Kanagawa - Care Center
サンシティ神奈川 - ケアセンター

四季の変化を感ずる東京近郊のケアセンター
The Care Center, located in an urban area nearby to Tokyo, emphasizes the importance of the four seasons and natural light.

左上）居室に沿った共用部廊下、右上）食事やアクティビティのための温室、左下）大きな窓のある個室、右下）共用部の居間（写真：ジェイム・アルティル - アーセ）
Left above) Single-loaded corridor; windows on left are from resident rooms overlooking common activities and "neighborhood"; right above) "Greenhouse" areas contain dining, activities and gardening; left below) Single-resident Room with large window overlooking bird garden; right below) Living Room with comfortable, age-appropriate furnishings and lighting (photo: Jaime Ardiles-Arce)

34床のナーシングベッドと6床のハイケアベッドのあるこのケアセンターは、東京近郊にある終身介護施設の一部である。季節感を重視し、居住者の生活のための自然光に恵まれるように設計した。このため、居室の大きな開閉式の窓や自然光の入るトイレ、石庭や野鳥が棲息する森への眺望、食事やアクティビティ、園芸などを行う「温室」などを設えた。居室の廊下側にある窓は居室に明るさをもたらすと共に「コミュニティ」の感覚を強めることに役立っている。構造システムを活かしながら、ベッドを隣り合わせではなく互い違いに配することで、2人部屋でのプライバシーを高めている。これらの結果、開放的で明るく、活気あるケアセンターとなっている。

普通は気にされない換気シャフトを積極的に石庭とすることで、アメニティとアクティビティのための明るい領域を創出している。
カジュアルダイニングやミーティングルーム、ゲームや読書、会話のためのエリア、グループアクティビティ、「お風呂」などでは、居住者は生活を楽しむことができる。医療や運営を妨げない程度に、住宅用の仕上げを施すことで、「施設」らしからぬ雰囲気となっている。壁装材や木材、仕上げ材や家具は、居住者がかつて住んでいた家を想い起こさせる。高齢者にとって快適な明るさの色彩やパターンを基調とするデザインに使用されている素材は手入れがしやすく、また館内表示もわかりやすいものとなっている。

This is the Care Center component of a larger CCRC located nearby to Tokyo, and is composed of 34 Skilled Nursing beds and 6 High Care beds. The design emphasizes the importance of the four seasons and natural light in the harmony of the resident's daily life. This emphasis is accomplished through the large operable window in each resident room, natural light in the resident toilet room, an internal meditative rock garden, the lounge which views into a specially designed bird garden, and "greenhouse" common rooms that multi-function for dining, activities and planting. Enhancing the sense of "community", plus bringing light deep into the unit, is the internal window in each resident room that overlooks the single-loaded corridor system. Advantage was taken of the inherited structural system by planning resident rooms with foot-to-foot rather than side-by-side arrangement of beds, thus increasing privacy and a "zone" of personal ownership in the shared room. The result of these considerations is an open, bright and active Care Center.

By designing the passive rock garden within the required and typically-ignored ventilation shaft, an amenity was created and a source of mediation and light was provided for the Care Center around which many of the activities congregate.

Other common areas that contribute to the daily diversity of the residents include: casual dining, meeting rooms, games/reading/conversation areas, group activities and the conventional Japanese "ofuro" (bathing room) that has been especially designed for the needs of the elderly. Use of conventionally residential materials that meet healthcare and operational standards further contributes to this non-institutional environment. Wallcoverings, wood materials, finishes and furniture evoke memories of residents' previous homes. Colors emphasize lightness and simplicity, and the design accommodates the unique needs of the elderly: appropriate lighting levels, simple patterns, easily maintained finishes and clear graphics.

上）居間を望むアクティビティと多機能室、下）ゆったりと置かれたベッドのある2人部屋
（写真：ジェイム・アルティル‐アーセ）
Above) Activities and Multipurpose Room overlooking Living Room; below) Two-resident Room permits generous foot-to-foot arrangement of beds (photo: Jaime Ardiles-Arce)

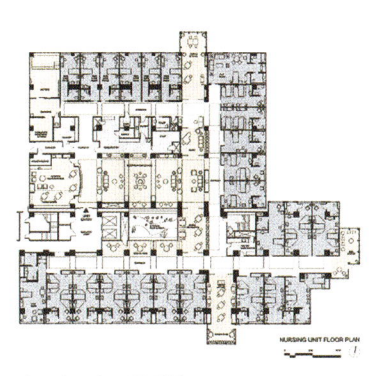

ケアセンター平面図
Care Center floor plan

ゲームエリア（写真：ジェイム・アルティル‐アーセ）
Small game area (photo: Jaime Ardiles-Arce)

Location: Hadano-shi, Kanagawa Japan
Completion: 1996
Site Area: 20,396.27 sqm
Gross Floor Area: 4,100 sqm
Height: 1 story
Structure: Steel Concrete structure
Number of Rooms: 34 skilled nursing beds and 6 high-care beds
Finishes:
<Predominant Exterior Wall>
 Tile and Glass
<Main lobby>
 Floor: Stone and Carpet
 Wall: Vinyl Wall Covering and Wood
 Ceiling: Gypsum Wallboard
Award: Winner, 1st Place, Symposium on Health Care Design, 1998

Client: Half Century More Co., Ltd.
Architect for Schematic Design: HOK/San Francisco and Tokyo
 (Alex Bonutti, AIA and Dennis Cope, AIA)
Architect for Design Development: Nippon Kokudo Kaihatsu Co., Ltd.
Interior Designer: HOK/San Francisco and Tokyo
 (Joyce Polhamus and Dennis Cope, AIA)
Landscape Designer: SWA Group
Predominant Contractor: Nippon Kokudo Kaihatsu Co., Ltd.

Royal Life Tama
ロイヤルライフ多摩

贅沢を楽しむ快適空間と設備、豊かな自然環境の理想の住まい
An ideal home with comfortable space and equipment for luxurious life within rich surrounding natural environment.

大きな庇のある玄関ポーチ
Entrance poach with a large canopy

東京の西郊外、多摩丘陵の豊かな自然の中に悠然と展開するロイヤルライフ多摩は、健常者用施設と要介護者用施設からなる複合老人居住施設である。
幹線道路から車で丘を上りつめると、東側に丘陵地帯の風景を望むメインエントランスに達する。滝の流れや鯉の群れる池、東屋が設えられた日本庭園に面するエントランスロビーや、南側に大きく張り出したラウンジなどの共用部は、どれもがゆとりある広さで、大きなガラス窓を通して見える緑や自然の光で明るく照らされている。
全ての居室は敷地の南斜面を活かして配置されており、そこには陽が射し込み涼風が通りぬける。またバルコニー越しに見える四季折々に変化する自然の景観も見事なものである。
後から増築された介護棟は明るい黄色の色調で仕上げられている他、アートセラピーのための壁飾りが居住者をなごませる。ここでは安全性を高めるために、先端的なセキュリティシステムが導入されている。

Campus of the Royal Life Tama, housing independent, care and nursing units, is developed midst natural environment of Tama hills.
Residents reach to main entrance from a public street by car though gentle slope and look over spectacular scenery of the hills on east. Spacious public areas such as main lobby looking down Japanese style garden with Koi pond, cascade and arbor and central lounge extending to environment on the south are lit from natural sun light.
Resident rooms on this hilly site with slope to south are distributed natural light and gentle breeze. Thorough balcony of rooms, residents enjoy to see and feel seasonal view of surrounding environment.
Aiming to create of comfortable facility, expanded nursing home, finished with light yellow color, is ornamented with pictures for art-therapy along with advanced security system.

植栽が施された介護棟の屋上庭園
Roof garden, care building

Client: Ryomei Royal Life Co., Ltd.
Master Designer: Mitsubishi jisho Co., Ltd.
Architect for Schematic Design: Mitsubishi jisho Co., Ltd.
Architect for Design Development: Mitsubishi jisho Co., Ltd.
Predominant Contractor: Fujita Co., Ltd

アプローチからの外観（写真：中島悠二）
Exterior view from approach (photo: Yuji Nakajima)

多摩丘陵という豊かな自然に恵まれている立地条件を活かし、どの居室からでも採光と眺望を楽しめるように工夫され、ロビーやラウンジをはじめ廊下を含めて共用部から十分に景観を楽しめるように設計されている。

入居者のだれでもが使える共用施設は充実しており、その割合は全居室面積を合わせた広さと共用部の全面積とが1:1となっている。できるだけ居室にこもらず日常を共用部でゆったり過ごせるための工夫がなされている。

Condition of this site, surrounded by rich natural environment called as Tamakyuryou, enables all of resident rooms to enjoy natural sunlight and spectacular view. And buildings and public areas are discretely allocated to look over scenery. Spacious public area resulting from fifty percent of gross floor area leads residents to be out of their rooms and enjoy public life with comfort.

居室の入口がセットバックした介護棟の廊下（写真：中島悠二）
Public corridor, care building (photo: Yuji Nakajima)

介護棟のアートセラピー（写真：中島悠二）
Art therapy, care building (photo: Yuji Nakajima)

介護棟外観
Exterior view, care building

丘の眺望が大きく開けるメインロビー
Main lobby with view of hill

玄関脇に置かれたモニュメント「多摩の丘」
(写真：中島悠二)
Tamano-oka sculpture at main entry
(photo: Yuji Nakajima)

広々としたダイニングルーム
Dining room

ロイヤルライフ多摩　143

茶室
Tea house

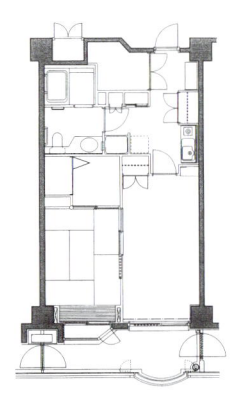

居室平面図
Unit plan

ジャグジーのある大浴場
Communal bath

庭園のレンダリング
Rendering of garden

庭園
Garden

配置図
Site plan

ロビー・居室階平面図
Lobby and resident room floor plan

落ち着いた雰囲気の居室
Comfortable resident room

Location: Machida-shi, Tokyo Japan
Completion: 1991
Renovation/Extension: 2004 (extension of nursing building)
Site Area: 26,822 sqm
Gross Floor Area: 16,523 sqm
Height: Under ground 1 story; Above ground 6 stories
Structure: Reinforced Concrete structure
Number of Rooms: 164 rooms
Parking: 35 cars
Finishes:
<Predominant Exterior Wall>
	Ceramic Tile
<Main lobby>
	Floor: Carpet
	Wall: Wall Covering
	Ceiling: Wall Covering

中庭へと開かれた明るい雰囲気の受付ロビー
Reception lobby with natural light

The Hamilton

ザ・ハミルトン

パロアルトの建築様式とアメニティとを融合した高級コンドミニアム
Luxury senior condominiums responding to architecture and amenity of Palo Alto.

交差点からの眺め（写真：ドゥグ・ダン、BAR アーキテクツ）
Hamilton Avenue at Middlefield Road (photo: Doug Dun / BAR Architects)

ザ・ハミルトンはパロアルトの伝統的な建築様式を尊重した古典的なデザインとアメニティとを融合した高齢者向けの高級コンドミニアムである。それは近隣の環境と調和しながら、街の中心の近くに位置している。いくつかの寝室がある大きな住戸には、通りに面する専用の出入口や中庭を見下ろすテラスがある。特にゆとりある広さの4階の住戸では、都市生活の利便性と贅沢さを享受できるように配慮されている。ライブラリーやダイニングルーム、レクリエーション施設、フィットネスセンター、屋内プールなどの共用施設がある1階の下には駐車場がある。2つのビジター用の部屋があることで居住者の快適性はさらに高まる。この高密度な4階建ての建物が街の雰囲気に巧みに織り込まれるように、建物のプロポーションと外構計画を特に慎重に検討した。

This luxurious condominium project for senior citizens combines classical design and amenities to capture the graciousness of traditional California architecture. Located immediately adjacent to downtown Palo Alto, the building responds to its surroundings in a formal yet familiar manner. Spacious two-and three-bedroom units capitalize on adjacency to the street with private entries and terraces overlooking formal courtyards. Special attention was given to the generous fourth floor units to provide the most luxurious urban living experience possible. Below grade parking frees the ground level for the common facilities: a library, dining room, activities room, fitness center and indoor lap pool. Two guest suites complete the amenities available for the residents. Careful proportions and sensitive landscaping enable this high-density, four-story building to be woven gracefully into the existing urban fabric.

中庭のロッジア（写真：ドゥグ・ダン、BAR アーキテクツ）
Loggia at courtyard (photo: Doug Dun / BAR Architects)

正面玄関（写真：ドゥグ・ダン、BAR アーキテクツ）
Main entry (photo: Doug Dun / BAR Architects)

Client: Hamilton Avenue Properties
Master Designer: BAR Architects
Architect for Schematic Design: BAR Architects
Architect for Design Development: The Ratcliff Architects
    (The Ratcliff Architects - Architect of Record)
Interior Designer: Schroeder & Grant
Landscape Designer: Emery Rogers and Associates
Predominant Contractor: Vance M. Brown and Sons

住戸の居間（写真：ドゥグ・ダン、BAR アーキテクツ）
Residential living room (photo: Doug Dun / BAR Architects)

住戸の書斎と主寝室（写真：ドゥグ・ダン、BAR アーキテクツ）
Sitting area and master bedroom (photo: Doug Dun / BAR Architects)

住戸の主寝室（写真：ドゥグ・ダン、BAR アーキテクツ）
Residential master bedroom (photo: Doug Dun / BAR Architects)

The Hamilton

木構造の露出した共用部の居間（写真：ドゥグ・ダン、BAR アーキテクツ）
Common living room (photo: Doug Dun / BAR Architects)

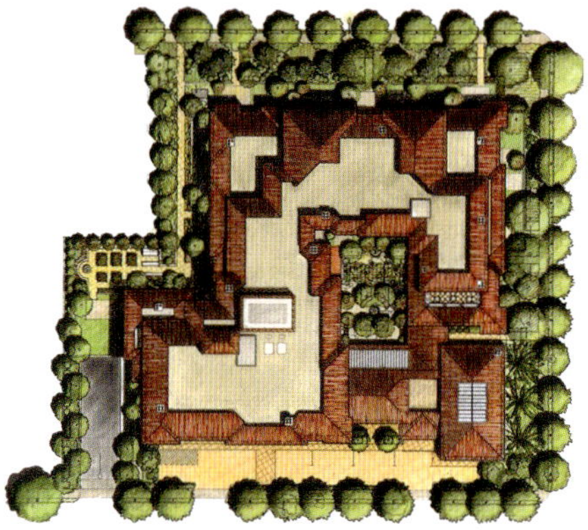

配置図
Site plan

1階平面図
Ground floor plan

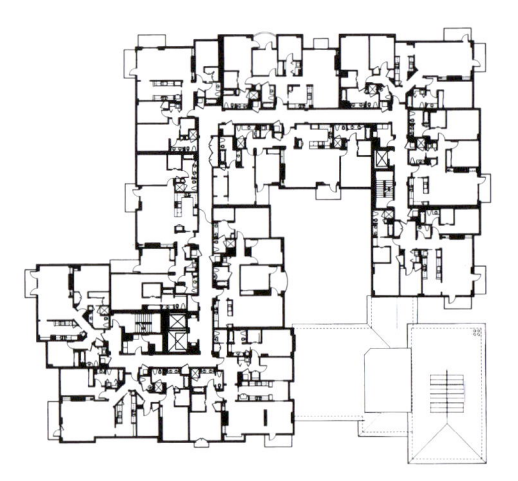

居室階平面図
Residents room floor plan

居室平面図
Unit plan

ハミルトン通りからの眺め（写真：ドゥグ・ダン、BAR アーキテクツ）
Hamilton Avenue street view (photo: Doug Dun / BAR Architects)

Location: Palo Alto, CA U.S.A.
Completion: 1992
Site Area: 4,860 sqm
Gross Floor Area: 7,990 sqm
Height: Under ground 1 story; Above ground 4 stories
Structure: Concrete structure
Number of Rooms: 36 rooms
Parking: 73 cars
Finishes:
<Predominant Exterior Wall>
    Cement Plaster
<Main lobby>
    Floor: Stone
    Wall: Plaster
    Ceiling: Plaster with Wood Trim

ロビーと受付廻り（写真：ドゥグ・ダン、BAR アーキテクツ）
Lobby and reception area (photo: Doug Dun / BAR Architects)

スイミングプール（写真：ドゥグ・ダン、BAR アーキテクツ）
Swimming pool (photo: Doug Dun / BAR Architects)

ライブラリー（写真：ドゥグ・ダン、BAR アーキテクツ）
Common library (photo: Doug Dun / BAR Architects)

Seashore Gardens Living Center
シーショアガーデンズ・リビングセンター

栄光の1940年代のクラシックなリゾートを想わせる高齢者居住施設
A Senior Living Facility with character of this classic seashore resort during its heyday in the late 1940s.

60年代の壁画 (1940年代のアトランティック・シティ) のあるヘルスケアセンターのボードウォークピア・ラウンジ (写真：トム・ベルナルド・フォトグラフィ)
Boardwalk Pier Lounge with 60' vintage mural (Atlantic City circa 1940's) - Healthcare Center(photo: Tom Bernard Photography)

シーショアガーデンズはニュージャージー州のアトランティック・シティのボードウォークに100年程前に誕生した。ボードウォークの敷地にあるこの施設の改修が難しいことが計画段階の初期に明らかになったので、代わりにギャロウェイタウンシップの陸側に16kmほど入った所の土地を開発することとなった。新しい高齢者介護のためのキャンパスは約80,000平方メートルの森の中に位置している。キャンパスは151床の介護施設と30室の介助施設から構成されており、将来、アダルト・デイケアと健常棟もここに設置されることになっている。

居住者の生活の質を高めるために建物には多くの共用部がある。また、家に居るようなスケールとなるように個性的なエリアが設定された。各エリアはそれぞれのテーマによってデザインが施されており、居室群やパティオ、2階にポーチのある居間からなっている。

アトランティック・シティといえば、穏やかな夏の夜の散策、大西洋への眺望と壮観なアミューズメントピア、美味しい食事などを思い浮かべる。経験豊かな非営利目的の事業者による、このユダヤ人のためのナーシングホームはここでそれを成し遂げた。

栄光の1940年代のこの伝統的な海浜リゾートならではのスケールやディテール、特徴を再現するために設計段階で入念な検討が行われ、パイプレールのあるボードウォークや商店、当時の浜辺と有名な桟橋を描いた15メートルの壁画を設えた。介護施設ではアトランティック・シティのコスモポリタンホテルを参考にした。多くのディテールやモチーフがその歴史的建物を参考にしている。この最先端の施設であるシーショアガーデンズ・リビングセンターは、いまだに「浜辺の一角」に建っているかのように思える。社長兼CEOのマーチン・クラインは、居住者がアトランティック・シティから転居しても、相変わらず元の場所に居るかのように思うだろうと考えている。

中庭と鯉の池（写真：トム・ベルナルド・フォトグラフィ）
Courtyard & Koy Fish Pond (photo: Tom Bernard Photography)

For close to a century, Seashore Gardens was located on the Boardwalk in Atlantic City, New Jersey. Early in the planning stages, it became clear that redevelopment of the home's Boardwalk site would be problematic, and it was decided to develop a parcel of land approximately 10 miles inland in Galloway Township. The new senior-care campus is located on a 20-acre wooded site. The campus consists of a 151-bed skilled nursing facility and a 30-apartment assisted living facility; future expansion will include Adult Day Care and Independent Living buildings.

The building has a tremendous amount of public space, which enhances residents' quality of life. Also, distinct neighborhoods were established to provide a more homelike scale. Each neighborhood has a separate theme or decor, containing a cluster of rooms and Living Room with either a patio or second-floor porch.

Remember Atlantic City? ...strolling along the boards on a warm summer night ...looking out at the Atlantic Ocean and the spectacular amusement piers ...eating all of your favorite foods? This well-established nonprofit Jewish nursing home certainly did. Martin Klein, President & CEO, felt that even though the residents had to be moved, they did not have to leave Atlantic City. Every effort was taken in designing and furnishing these spaces to recall the scale, detailing, and character of this classic seashore resort during its heyday in the late 1940s. There is an actual boardwalk with pipe rail, shops, and even a 45-foot mural featuring the beach and famous piers of the day. The Assisted Living facility was modeled after the original structure in Atlantic City, the Cosmopolitan Hotel. Many of the details and motifs were borrowed from that historic building. The new Seashore Gardens Living Center is a state-of-the-art facility and is still on the "beach block"!

Client: Seashore Gardens, Atlantic City, New Jersey
Architect for Schematic Design: Kanalstein Danton Associates, P.A.
Architect for Design Development: Kanalstein Danton Associates, P.A.
Interior Designer: Merlino Design Partnership, Inc.
Owner Representative Consultant: RFC Consulting - Rich Casamento
Predominant Contractor: LF Driscoll Construction Company

アールデコ調の介助棟の大階段（写真：トム・ベルナルド・フォトグラフィ）
Art Deco Styled Grand Staircase - Assisted Living (photo: Tom Bernard Photography)

受付デスクと大階段
Reception desk and Ground staircase

マーチン・クライン社長兼CEOのコメント

我々は単なるナーシングホームでなく、本当の家のようなものを創ろうとした。例えば目障りなナースコールや、扉の上や居室の入口の照明器具がない。薬品庫や医療・給食サービス、機器、日用品などは、目につかないようにナースステーションの机の後ろにある。居室の入口を廊下から凹ませることで、住宅のような雰囲気を出している。二重の隠し扉がある廊下は居住者の快適さと利便性のために短くしてある。低めに設定された窓には居住者が装飾品を置けるように幅広の窓台がある。

ボードウォークの側には、居間の周りに配された5つの居室からなるこの長期介護のためのエリアがあり、その反対側には、ワンベッドルームやツーベッドルームの介護付アパートメントがある。エリアの設えはユニークであり、例えば、フレンチクォーターには1930年代のパリを描いた大きな絵画があり、シーサイド・エリアには海をテーマとし浜辺の絵がある。アールデコをテーマとしている介護付居室部分は薄いピンク色と明るい木目を特徴としている。長期介護施設側には、居住者が記念品を置くための浅い箱が部屋の外にあり、介護付居室には棚がある。各階に配された保管倉庫が介護棟の各居住者に割り当てられている。居住者は自分の電話番号を持っており、全ての部屋にはコンピュータ用の配線が施されている。

いくつかの中庭や2.5層分の吹き抜けによって、居室や廊下は自然光が入って明るい。また全てのダイニングルームは少なくとも一面が外部に面している。飼鳥園や水槽が特徴のアトリウムには、ライブラリーやチャペル、フィットネスセンター、カフェ、子供のプレイエリア、ギフトショップなどがある。長期介護施設には認知症ユニットがある。厨房や食卓、専用庭、ラウンジ、メディテーションルームがあり、それはまさに家のようである。ダイニングルームの外にも庭があり、そこには魚が泳ぐ池へと水が流れる水路がある。また、散策路が施設全体の周囲を巡っている。

新しい施設の成功を重ねることは実に喜ばしいことである。ある居住者の娘さんが、親戚を手招きしながら、「母の家のようなものを見せてあげる」と言いながらボードウォークに立っていた。そのことはこれが本当の家であることを語っている。

ADMINISTRATOR'S COMMENTS

Martin Klein, President and CEO:

"We've tried to create something other than a nursing home here-an actual home. For example, there is no visible nurse call system, and there are no lights over doors or room entrances. The drug room and all medical/dietary services, equipment, and supplies are out of sight, behind the desk that serves as the only visible nurses' station. A more residential look also has been achieved by recessing the entrances to the residents' rooms, so that they aren't flush with the hallway. The hallways themselves were kept short for the comfort and convenience of residents, and there are only concealed double doors. Windows are low, with wide sills where residents can display decorative items.

"Our long-term care 'neighborhoods'-each of which consists of five resident rooms built around a living room-are on one side of the Boardwalk, and the one- and two-bedroom assisted living apartments are on the other side. Each LTC neighborhood is uniquely decorated. For example, the French Quarter has large pictures depicting Paris in the 1930s, and the Seaside neighborhood has an ocean theme and beach pictures. The assisted living area has an art deco theme, featuring medium cherry and light wood finishes. On the LTC side, residents have shadowboxes outside their rooms for displaying memorabilia, and on the assisted living side they have shelves. AL residents also have their own secure storage areas, conveniently located on each floor. Every resident throughout the facility has his or her own phone number, and all rooms are wired for computers.

"The 2 1/2-story atrium, along with several courtyards throughout the facility, allow ample natural light into the rooms and hallways. All the dining rooms have at least one outside wall for this purpose, as well. The atrium features an aviary and aquarium. We also have a library, chapel, fitness center, cafe, children's play area, and gift shop.

"Within the long-term care facility is a certified dementia unit. It's very homey, with a kitchen area, congregate dining, its own park, a lounge, and a meditation room. There are also park areas outside the rest of the facility's dining rooms, and we have a man-made creek that flows to a fish-filled pond. Walking paths wind around the entire facility.

"I witnessed something recently that, to me, sums up the success our new facility is enjoying: A daughter of one of our residents was standing on our Boardwalk, waving to her relatives and saying, 'Let me show you what Mom's home looks like.' That tells me it really is home."

歴史的な写真のあるヘルスケアセンターのボードウォークの吹き抜け
（写真：トム・ベルナルド・フォトグラフィ）
Boardwalk Atrium with Historic Photography - Healthcare Center (photo: Tom Bernard Photography)

ヘルスケアセンターの正面玄関と車寄せ（写真：トム・ベルナルド・フォトグラフィ）
Front Entrance & Porte Cochere - Healthcare (photo: Tom Bernard Photography)

Seashore Gardens Living Center

ヘルスケアセンターのボードウォークカフェ（写真：トム・ベルナルド・フォトグラフィ）
Boardwalk Cafe - Healthcare Center (photo: Tom Bernard Photography)

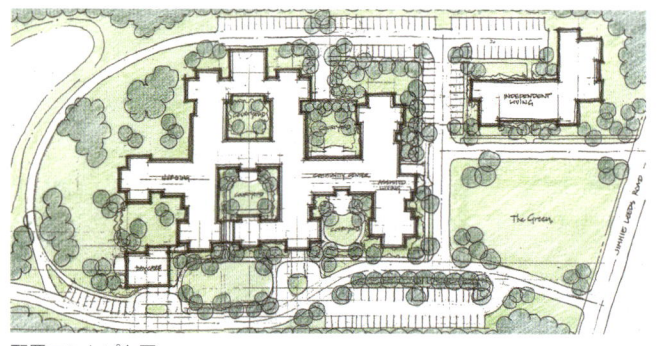

配置コンセプト図
Conceptual site plan

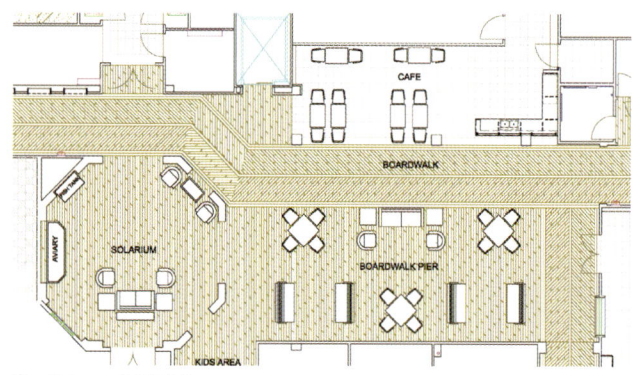

ボードウォーク平面図
Boardwalk plan

ボードウォークカフェ展開図
Boardwalk Cafe elevation

ライブラリーとクラブルーム、ダイニングルーム
（写真：トム・ベルナルド・フォトグラフィ）
Library, Club room and Dining room
(photo: Tom Bernard Photography)

ヘルスケアセンターのナースステーションとバルコニー
（写真：トム・ベルナルド・フォトグラフィ）
Nurse's Station & Balcony - Healthcare Center
(photo: Tom Bernard Photography)

Location: Galloway Township, New Jersey U.S.A.
Completion: 2003
Site Area: 80,970 sqm
Gross Floor Area: 11,730 sqm
Height: 2 stories
Structure: Steel and Concrete structure
Number of Rooms:
    30 Assisted Living apartments
    121 Skilled Nursing
    30 Special Care
Parking: On Grade Parking
Finishes:
<Predominant Exterior Wall>
    Vinyl Siding, Wood Trim and Asphalt Shingle Roof
<Main lobby>
    Floor: Vinyl Boardwalk Plank and Carpet
    Wall: Vinyl Wall Covering
    Ceiling: Acoustic Ceiling Tile / GWB Soffits
Award: Long Term Care Magazine, Design Center Featured Project, Seashore Gardens Living Center, May 2003; Design for Senior Environments, 2003 Published Project, Seashore Gardens Living Center, March 2003

介助棟の居住部分の廊下（写真：トム・ベルナルド・フォトグラフィ）
Resident Corridor - Assisted Living (photo: Tom Bernard Photography)

ヘルスケアセンターの居住部分の廊下と居間
（写真：トム・ベルナルド・フォトグラフィ）
Resident Corridor & Living Room - Healthcare Center
(photo: Tom Bernard Photography)

介助棟のロビー（写真：トム・ベルナルド・フォトグラフィ）
Lobby - Assisted Living (photo: Tom Bernard Photography)

介助棟のメイン・ダイニングルーム（写真：トム・ベルナルド・フォトグラフィ）
Main Dining Room - Assisted Living (photo: Tom Bernard Photography)

Seashore Gardens Living Center

Elegano Konan
エレガーノ甲南

女性インテリアデザイナーによる優美な空間演出
Elegant environment coordinated by a female interior designer

メインロビー
Main Lobby

阪神間の閑静な住宅地として人気の高い、神戸市東灘区本山地区に立地する介護付有料老人ホームで、建物はパティオを中心に、一般棟、ケアセンター棟の2棟で構成され、多様化する高齢者ニーズにこたえる居住空間を備えている。一般棟は終身利用権方式の一般住戸105戸で構成、ケアセンター棟は介護に応じたユニットケア方式を採用し、介護居室97室および一時介護室3室で構成している。

共用部にはメインダイニング、多目的ホール、サロン、ライブラリー、天然温泉利用の大浴場など充実した生活サポート施設を備えている。医療・健康管理面のサポート機能として、クリニック、リハビリテーションルーム、屋外リハビリガーデンなどを備えている。共用部の内装・照明・家具は米国の女性インテリアデザイナーが基本設計を担当し、「アットホーム・女性的・優美」を基本テーマにカントリーフレンチ調で統一された格調の高いインテリア空間を意図してつくられている。

メインダイニング
Main Dining Room

Located Motoyama-chiku at Nada-ku in Kobe-shi, a popular area as gentle residential area between Osaka and Kobe, the Elegano Konan accommodates Independent Living facility and Care Center within two buildings surrounding a patio to correspond to variable needs of senior citizen. The Independent Living facility houses 105 rooms for life-long, and the Care Center providing the Unit Care corresponding to level of care with residents dose 97 care units and 3 temporal care units.

In common area, dining room, multi purpose room, saloon, library, and communal bath using natural hot spring support life of residents as well as clinic, rehabilitation room, outdoor rehabilitation garden support health care of them. Through collaboration with female American interior designer during basic design phase for interiors, lighting and furniture at common area, elegant interior space with hotel taste in country French style was created by following basic concept of "At home, Female and Elegant".

共用部の廊下
Corridor at Common Area

ラウンジ
Lounge

居室
Residents Room

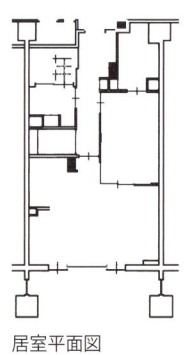

居室平面図
Residents room plan

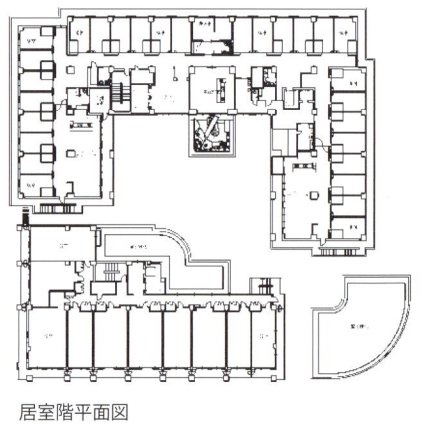

居室階平面図
Residnets room floorplan

外観
Exterior view

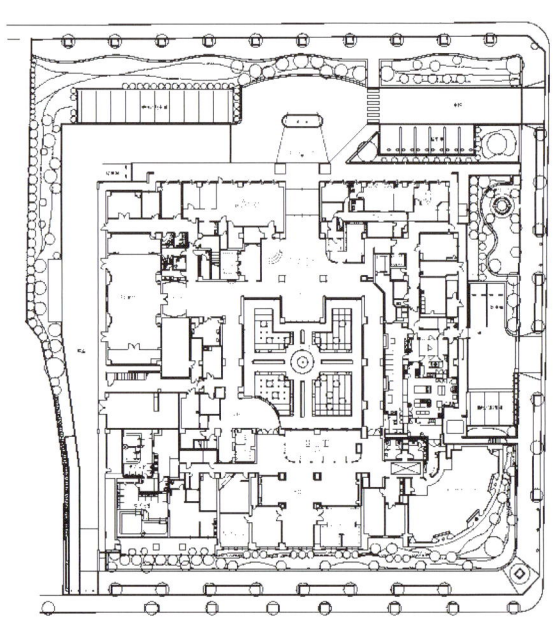

1階平面図
1st floor plan

160 エレガーノ甲南

サロンの談話コーナー
Seating Area at Saloon

Client: Shinko Care Life Co., Ltd
Architect for Schematic Design: Obayashi Corporation
Architect for Design Development: Obayashi Corporation
Interior Designer (Basic Design): Rita.St.Clair.Associates inc.
Predominant Contractor:
    Obayashigumi and Shinko Kosan Kensetsu J.V.

Location: Kobe-shi, Hyogo
Completion: 2006
Site Area: 7,889 sqm
Gross Floor Area: 19,061 sqm
Height: Above ground 14 stories, and Above ground 6 stories
Structure: Concrete structure
Number of Rooms:
    105 independent living units
    97 care units + 3 temporal units
Parking: 47 cars
Finishes:
<Predominant Exterior Wall>
    Ceramic Tile
<Main lobby>
    Floor: Tile and Marble Stone
    Wall: Wall Covering
    Ceiling: Wall Covering

サロン
Saloon

エレガーノ甲南

Newbury Court Retirement Community
ニューベリーコート・リタイアメントコミュニティ

渓谷を見下ろす立地と歴史的建築による意匠のコミュニティ
Retirement Community Upscale Housing overlooking the river with detailing of the area's Colonial and Georgian architectural heritage.

保全されたオークと建物の背後（写真：ハッチンス・フォトグラフィ）
Rear with Preserved Oak (photo: Hutchins Photography)

ニューベリーコート・リタイアメントコミュニティは、コロニアル時代とジョージア時代の建築のディテールや、レンガや石材、ファイバーグラスで成形された木工製品、錬鉄などを用いることで、マサチューセッツ州コンコード市の歴史性や文化性を表現している。川や草原への眺望を活かし自然に恵まれた敷地を保全することに配慮しながら、建物の位置や方向が検討された。建築家がデザインしたモールディングや天井の曲面、その他の歴史的要素など、複雑なディテールと共にインテリアでの工夫が凝らされている。

交流やレクリエーションのための主なエリアは、広大な芝生を見渡し渓谷を見下ろすダイニングルームがある1階にある。居室階では中央にエレベーターを配し、渓谷への眺望と方向感のあるラウンジがあるロビーが特徴である。短い廊下によってクラスターの効果が発揮され、そこには多くの理想的なコーナーユニットが配されている。

2つの低層階には、駐車場と川を望むエキソサイズセンター、理美容室、木工室、居住者用の倉庫がある。1階には交流／レクリエーション用の共用部、ダイニングルーム、居間／パーラー、多目的会議室、ギャラリー、表玄関のロビー、ラウンジ、ライブラリー、カフェ、プライバシーを確保したエレベーターロビー、メールルーム、ダイニングと居間の外の大きなテラス、カフェの外の小さなテラスや談話コーナーなどがある。

窓からの環境光はやわらかく、眩しさを軽減しながら十分な光が入るように設計されている。動線には方向性があり、全体的には居住者が威厳を感じることのできる雰囲気となっている。

航空写真（写真：ハッチンス・フォトグラフィ）
Arial View (photo: Hutchins Photography)

The Newbury Court Retirement Community structures exemplify the cultural heritage of historic Concord, MA, incorporating a blend of brick, stone, fiberglass molded millwork and wrought iron detailing in keeping with the area's Colonial and Georgian architectural heritage. Great care was taken to preserve the site in its natural state, while maximizing views of the river and meadows through building orientation and site placement. The intricate details carry into the interiors where the architect designed sculpted moldings, ceiling coves and other historically appropriate elements.

Main social and recreational areas are on the first floor, where the dining room overlooks a "great lawn" and river valley below. Lower levels contain "hard" activities and enclosed parking. A typical residential floor features a centrally located elevator and lobby with an adjacent lounge that provides views of the river valley and aids in orientation. Short corridors reinforce a cluster effect, while the overall shape and massing of the floor plan provides for many desirable corner units

The two lower levels contain parking, an exercise center overlooking the river, beauty shop, woodworking shops, and resident storage areas. The First Floor houses the primary social/recreational public spaces; Dining Rooms, Living Room/Parlor, Multi-Purpose Meeting Rooms, Galleries, Main Entrance Lobby, Lounge, Library, Cafe, a discreetly screened for privacy Elevator Lobby, Mail Room and other gathering spots including a Grand sweeping Terrace off the Dining & Living Rooms and a smaller intimate Terrace off the Cafe.

Ambient lighting, derived from an unusually large number of windows is softer and designed to reduce glare, yet also higher than is normally specified for conventional apartment buildings.

The circulation plan is simplified to aid orientation and the overall design is an environment that gives the senior resident a sense of dignity.

Client: New England Deaconess Association;
    Rev. Guy S. Morrison, President/CEO Emeritus
Architect: Tsomides Associates Architects Planners/TAAP
Master Designer: Constantine L. Tsomides, NCARB, AIA
    MArch, Columbia Univ; MDesS, Harvard GSD
Design Team: Francis W. Domurat, Najim Azadzoi, Thomas J. McBride,
    Diana G. Tsomides, Emily R. Huang
Interior Designer: Currier & Associates
Landscape Designer: John Wacker & Associates, Inc.
Predominant Contractor: Turner Construction Company

背面のテラス（写真：ハッチンス・フォトグラフィ）
Rear Terrace (photo: Hutchins Photography)

Location: Concord, MA U.S.A.
Completion: 1996
Site Area: 141,640 sqm
Gross Floor Area: 14,590 sqm
Height: Under ground 2 stories; Above ground 6 stories
Structure: Steel frame upper Six Stories
 Reinforced Concrete lower two stories (parking garage)
Number of Rooms: 573 rooms
Parking: 77 cars
Finishes:
<Predominant Exterior Wall>
 Brick and Precast Concrete
<Main lobby>
 Floor: Carpet
 Wall: Wall Covering and Paint
 Ceiling: Acoustic Tile and Drywall
Award: The Best of Seniors' Housing, National Council on Seniors' Housing, National Association of Home Builders, 1998; American Institute of Architects/ American Association of Homes and Services for the Aging, 1994; Design for Aging Review, 1994 (for project in Design Phase)
Publication: Featured in Urban land Institute book, "Seniors' Housing And Care Facilities; Development, Business,and Operation," by Paul A. Gordon. ULI 1998.

6階のエレベーター ロビーからの眺め（写真：ハッチンス・フォトグラフィ）
View from 6th Floor Elevator Lobby (photo: Hutchins Photography)

レンダリング 01（写真：フランク・コンスタンティン）
Rendering 01 (photo: Frank Constantin)

レンダリング 02（写真：フランク・コスタンティノ）
Rendering 02 (photo: Frank Costantino)

保全されたオークと建物の背後（写真：ハッチンス・フォトグラフィ）
Rear with Preserved Oak Tree (photo: Hutchins Photography)

表玄関（写真：ハッチンス・フォトグラフィ）
Main Entrance (photo: Hutchins Photography)

Newbury Court Retirement Community

表玄関のロビー（写真：ハッチンス・フォトグラフィ）
Main Entrance Lobby (photo: Hutchins Photography)

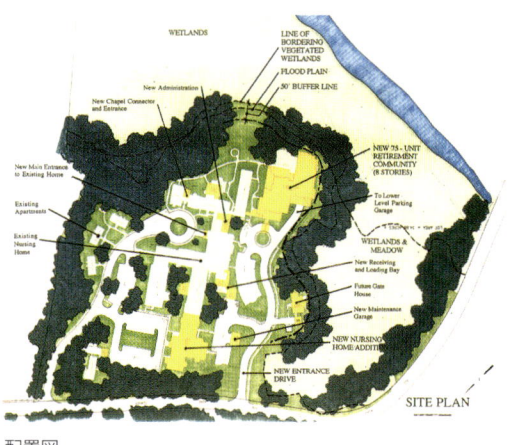

敷地の傾斜を利用して、駐車場を健常者用のユニットの下に配した。南ウィングの南西の角での雁行は、セットバックの規則によって生じた湿地でのバファーゾンでもある。健常棟と隣接する介護棟によって、ヒューマンスケールなランドスケープが施された庭ができている。また、居室階には7室のコーナーユニットがある。

居室平面図
Unit plan

住戸（写真：ハッチンス・フォトグラフィ）
Residents room (photo: Hutchins Photography)

配置図
Site plan

基準階平面図
Typical floor plan

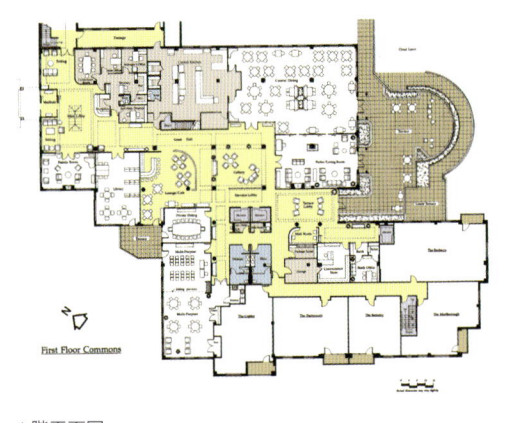

1階平面図
1st floor plan

The sloping site provided opportunity to place parking below the ILU structure. The southwest corner of the south wing and its jogged exterior wall is a result of the setback requirements of the wetlands buffer zone.

The shape and massing of the new ILU forms an intimate human scale landscaped courtyard with the adjacent residential care building while providing Seven desirable corner units on the typical residential floors.

166 Newbury Court Retirement Community

ダイニングルーム（写真：ハッチンス・フォトグラフィ）
Dining Room (photo: Hutchins Photography)

ギャラリー（写真：ハッチンス・フォトグラフィ）
Gallery (photo: Hutchins Photography)

ギャラリー（写真：ハッチンス・フォトグラフィ）
Gallery (photo: Hutchins Photography)

ラウンジカフェ（写真：ハッチンス・フォトグラフィ）
Lounge-Cafe (photo: Hutchins Photography)

Newbury Court Retirement Community 167

Geriatric Nursing Home

ゲリアトリック・ナーシングホーム

高齢者のためのフリーダムとル・コルビュジェの建築作法
Freedom for the elderly and building design with the tradition of Le Corbusier.

正面の共用部へと向かう北側のアプローチ（写真：アンジェロ・カウナット）
Approach on the north side (photo: Angelo Kaunat)

郊外の戸建住宅街に位置し19室の個室からなるこの小規模なナーシングホームは民間団体によって運営されている。その不整形な敷地には北側のクルドサックを通じてたどり着く。

異なる表情の2つのボリュームが、2度の角度で微妙に振られて配されており、各階で接続されている。

ほぼ正方形の建物には北側の駐車場からアクセスする。1階は管理部門と厨房、居室への出入口と上階への出入口などからなる共用部である。上の階にはいくつかの処置ユニットや、南に面するバルコニーのある個室がある。

細長い棟には、共用部や駐車場に面さないように配された個室・寝室ユニットがある。

ビジターの出入口は大きな庇によって視認性が高くなっており、また側面の少しへこんだ部分には職員や業者用の出入口がある。他にはポーチや管理室、庭に面するサニタリーがある。配膳カウンター付の厨房が西側にあり、南に面している談話室は1階の大部分を占めている。そこは、コルビュジェの建築作法による分離要素である自由に配された大階段や寝台用エレベーターの脇の上からの光、上部が開放されたチャペルによって構成されている。部屋の頂部まで届く湾曲した木製の赤い間仕切り壁は、この空間に色彩のアクセントを与えており、これが無ければ無味乾燥な雰囲気の空間である。天井まで届くガラスは建物の南側を覆っており、大きな庭園への視界を開いている。庭のテラスは、夏の屋外の談話室ともなる。

The small nursing house is managed by a private association. It has 19 single rooms and is situated in a suburban area with detached houses. The site in the form of a hook is accessible from the north via a cul-de-sac.

Two separate construction bodies that are defined by a different form and appearance, slightly shifted out of parallelism (by 2 degrees) at a distance between each other. Both are two-storey buildings and connected to each other at each storey.

The nearly square building is accessed from the northern side, the parking area. The ground floor houses the administration and kitchen and - integrated into the common area - the entrance to the living rooms and entrances to the upper floors of both sections. Above there are several treatment units and, facing south, some of the private rooms with balconies.

The long slim construction houses the majority of the private living/sleeping room units, arranged as one individual element facing away from the common area and the parking space.

The visitors' entrance is easily recognisable by its generous canopy; on the side and set back a little there is the entrance for staff and traders. The porch, the administration and sanitary rooms facing the forecourt complete the building. A multifunctional communication room opens up towards south, covering the main surface of the ground floor area only limited on the western side by the kitchen with serving counter. On the one hand it is structured by the main stairs that are positioned freely in the room and lit from above near the bed-sized lift and a little chapel opening up towards the top, a separating element in the tradition of Le Corbusier. Its red boundary wall with plywood paneling reaching the room top and swung in the shape of a parable, gives a conscious colourful accent to this hall that is otherwise designed in a very moderate way dominated by light design. The glazing reaching the ceiling covers the entire southern side and sliding elements give an open view of the big garden. In the summer period the covered terrace at garden level extends the communication room.

玄関の北東からの眺め（写真：アンジェロ・カウナット）
Entrance from northeast (photo: Angelo Kaunat)

Client: Sozialhilfeverb and Leibnits
Master Designer:
    Di Hubert Schuller, Ing. Heribert Altenbacher
Architect for Schematic Design:
    Di Hubert Schuller, Ing. Heribert Altenbacher
Architect for Design Development:
    Di Uschi Marzendorfer
    Di Peter Szammer
    Claudia Schmidt
    Josef Ebner
    Martin Pallier Rosenberger

上階の処置ユニットと居住ユニットへは、1階を見下ろせるギャラリーを通って行く。西側の部分へはガラスの談話室へと導く短いブリッジを渡って行く。個室を直線に配することで、それらは2つの側面を持つことができる。廊下側にはバッファーのための出入口ホールと浴室があり、その反対側は古木のあるプライベートガーデンに向いている。居室には、西日対策のために突き出た屋根のある大きなバルコニー(1階ではテラス)が付いている。東側からは、端部に避難階段のある通路から個室にアクセスする。スリムな鉄製の梁の架構によって支持されている2層分のフレームレスのガラスファサードは独立性を保っている。

建物は鉄筋コンクリートのビームやプレート、床によって構成されている。フレキシビリティと軽快さを表現するために大梁や耐力壁などの使用は避けられた。天井にまで届く間接光の帯は、居室の上に浮かんでいるように見える緩やかに傾斜した屋根を形づくっている。ガラスや木材からなる非耐力要素としてのファサードづくりや換気のために、柱は空間に自由に配されている。1階北側では、水平に貼られたスリムなダグラス松のスラットや窓、間接光などの要素が構成している。南側と西側ではガラスとプライウッドが使われている。

外部から見えるチャペルの赤い壁、青緑のリノリウムの床、浴室の通路側の壁のオレンジ色などは、微妙な色彩のアクセントとなっている。限られた種類の素材や色彩の使用によって、建物は穏やかでユニークな存在となっている。

内部構成と通路には特別な配慮が払われている。ガラス面の大胆な使用や広間への良好な視界、庭や正面広場は、普段は行動範囲が限られている高齢者の日常に変化をもたらしている。

1階の個室と中庭（写真：アンジェロ・カウナット）
First floor rooms yard (photo: Angelo Kaunat)

Location: Styria Austria
Completion: 1995
Site Area: 3,800 sqm
Gross Floor Area: 2,650 sqm
Height: Under ground 1 story; Above ground 2 stories
Structure: Steel and Concrete structure
Number of Rooms: 19 rooms
Parking: 10 cars
Finishes:
<Predominant Exterior Wall>
　　　Wood and Glass
<Main lobby>
　　　Floor: Parkett
　　　Wall: Gipskarton
　　　Ceiling: Gipskarton and Glass
Award: Geramb-Medal, Province of Styria, 1996

バルコニー南側の遮光スクリーン（写真：アンジェロ・カウナット）
Balcony south sunscreen (photo: Angelo Kaunat)

The treatment and living units on the upper floor are entered via a gallery from which the entire scenery of the ground floor can be overlooked. The crossing to the western section is a short bridge leading into the glazed communication room of this building section. In linear order the rooms are adjacent to both sides. All rooms have a hall-stand and a bathroom that build a buffer towards the aisle, the rooms are oriented towards private garden sections with old trees. They have spacious balconies (terraces in the ground floor) that are protected from the sun in the west by the roof jutting out on this side. The access to the individual rooms from the eastern side is a freely protruding footbridge with fire escape stairs at the ends. It does not completely reach the frameless glass facade covering the two floors which is supported by a construction of slim steel beams.

The construction system of both building sections is composed by reinforced concrete beams and plates and slabs. Girders and bearers have been avoided what gives flexibility and lightness. The continuous band of indirect light reaching the ceiling makes the slightly inclined roof seem to hover over the room. The columns freely arranged in the room make the facade, that is lined with glass and timber and ventilated from behind, a non-supporting fine membrane. At the northern side the horizontal encasing of slim Douglas pine slats forms one level with windows and indirect lights. On the southern and western facade glazing and Okumee plywood are alternating.

The red wall of the chapel that is also visible from the outside, the linoleum floor in blue-green and the orange colour of the exterior wall of the baths in the aisle area give moderate colour accents. The reduced use of different materials and colours supports the calm and uniform character of the building.

上部が開放されたチャペル（写真：アンジェロ・カウナット）
Lobby chapel (photo: Angelo Kaunat)

スカイライトとギャラリーのある１階ロビー（写真：アンジェロ・カウナット）
First floor lobby (photo: Angelo Kaunat)

The organisation of the interiors and the paths through the building have been treated with particular care: the generous use of glass surfaces and well-aimed views into the hall, both gardens and the forecourt are designed to bring a bit more diversion into the everyday life of the mainly infirm elderly people who have a limited radius of movement.

グランドフロアー平面図
Ground floor plan

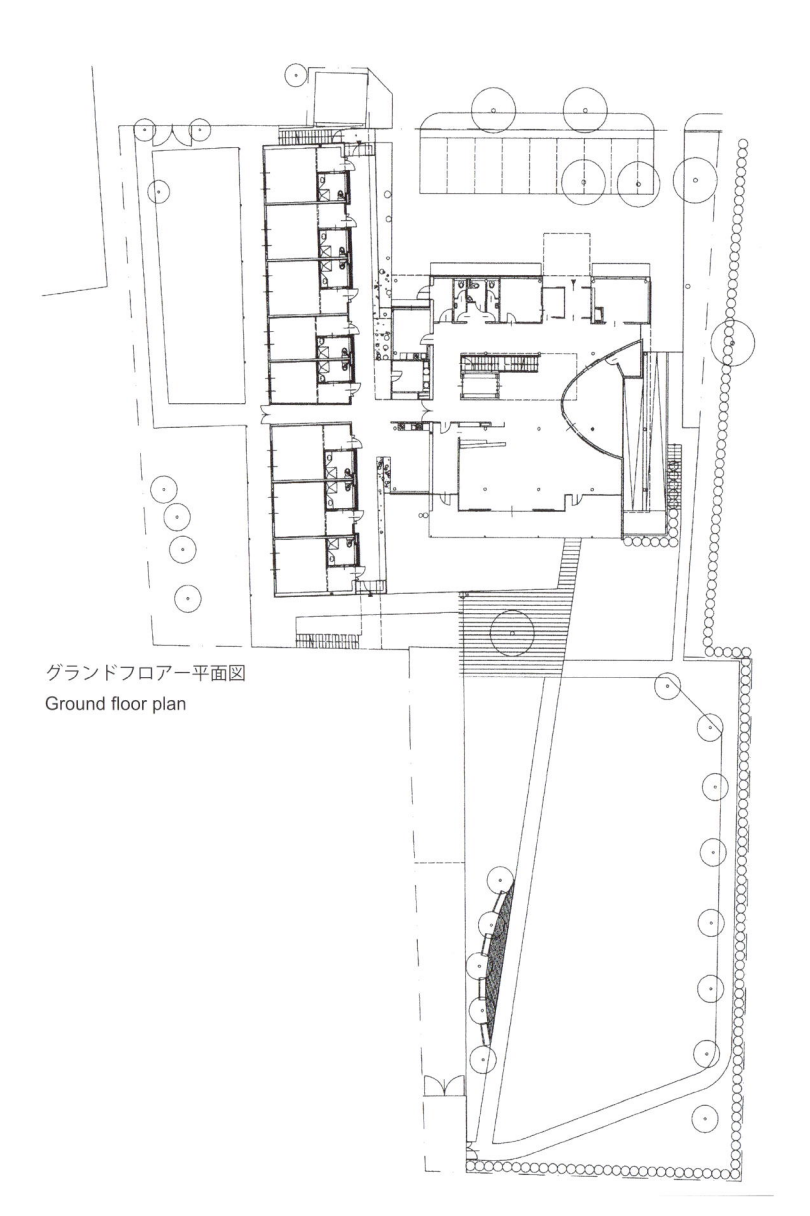

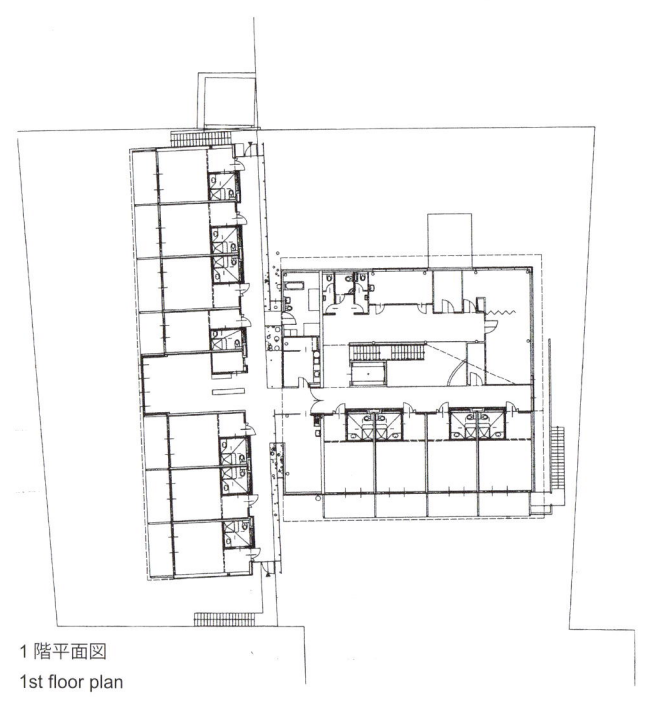

1 階平面図
1st floor plan

西側のバルコニー（写真：アンジェロ・カウナット）
Balcony west with a large roof above (photo: Angelo Kaunat)

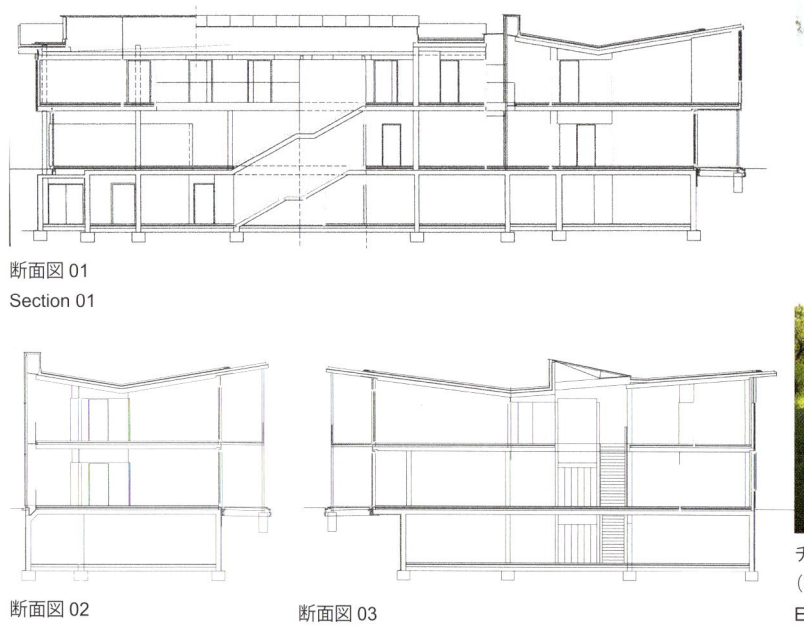

断面図 01
Section 01

断面図 02
Section 02

断面図 03
Section 03

チャペル東側の外観
（写真：アンジェロ・カウナット）
Exterior view of the chapel east
(photo: Angelo Kaunat)

1 階の中庭とサニタリー
（写真：アンジェロ・カウナット）
First floor rooms yard sanitary
(photo: Angelo Kaunat)

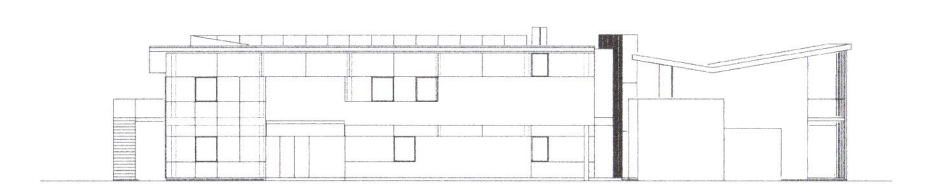

北立面図
North Elevation

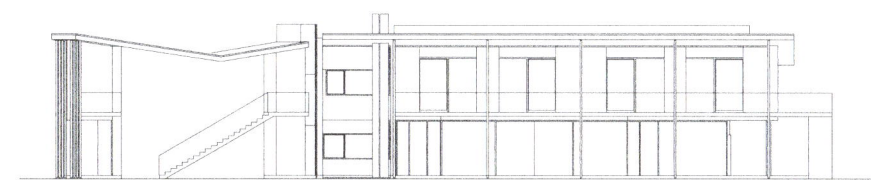

西立面図
West Elevation

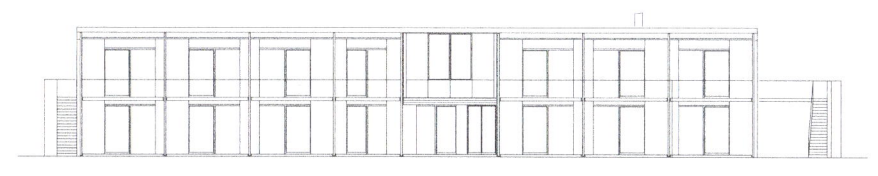

南立面図
South Elevation

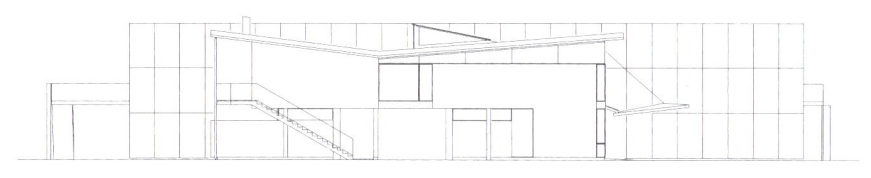

東立面図
East Elevation

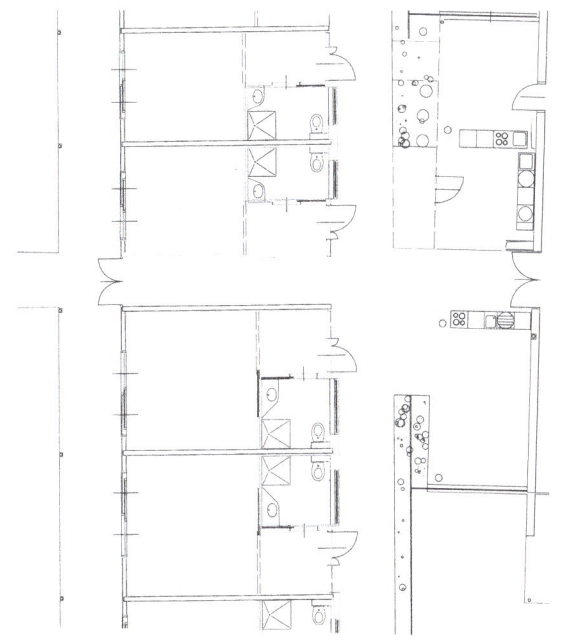

個室平面図
Typical unit plan

ガラスと木による正面玄関廻りの外観
（写真：アンジェロ・カウナット）
Entrance (photo: Angelo Kaunat)

チャペル（写真：アンジェロ・カウナット）
Lobby chapel (photo: Angelo Kaunat)

ロビーの大階段（写真：アンジェロ・カウナット）
Lobby main stair (photo: Angelo Kaunat)

Geriatric Nursing Home 173

Granda Syukugawa

グランダ夙川

都市近郊の高級住宅街に馴染む風情の施設
Facility for elderly, mildest of high-income area in Kansai.

周囲の邸宅に馴染む外観
Exterior view harmonious with surroundings

阪急神戸線夙川駅より徒歩8分の住宅地の中に、北向き斜面を背後に持つ敷地に建つ。エントランスから、ホールを通して中庭、背後の斜面につながる空間は2層吹抜けとなっており、広々とした開放感がある。上階の共用部がルーフバルコニーから後背斜面につながる空間となっており、豊かな緑を取り込んだ計画である。また、北側居室からは六甲山の雄大な景観を望むことができる。

This facility is built on a site, located eight minutes walking distance from Shukugawa station of Hankyu Kobe line, with a slope on the back of northern part. Spacious entrance has two stories atrium extending to court yard and the slope through hall. Public areas on upper levels introduce view of volume of surrounding green through roof balcony. Residents in north unit enjoy spectacular view of the Rokko Mountains.

Location: Koube-shi, Hyougo JAPAN
Completion: 2005
Site Area: 1,425 sqm
Gross Floor Area: 1,433 sqm
Height: 3 stories
Structure: Reinforced Concrete structure
Number of Rooms: 28 rooms
Parking: 5 cars
Finishes:
<Predominant Exterior Wall>
	Ceramic Tile and Exposed Concrete
<Main lobby>
	Floor: Ceramic Tile and Wood
	Wall: Vinyl Wall Covering and Ceramic Tile
	Ceiling: Vinyl Wall Covering

談話スペース（写真：杉野圭）
Seating area (photo: Kei Sugino)

Client: Benesse Style Care Co., Ltd.
Architect for Schematic Design: studio Void
Architect for Design Development: studio Void
Predominant Contractor: Maywa Koumuten, Ltd

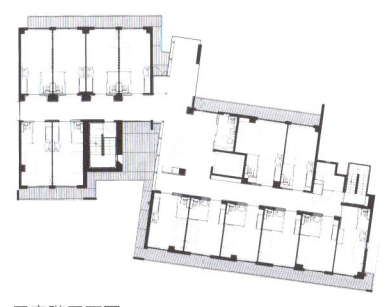

居室階平面図
Residents room floor plan

1階平面図
1st floor plan

ロビー（写真：杉野圭）
Lobby (photo: Kei Sugino)

グランダ夙川　175

Sun City Takarazuka
サンシティ宝塚

関西屈指の高級住宅地に展開するラグジュアリーなシニアリビング
Mountainside independent senior luxury living/CCRC overlooking Osaka.

コートヤード側のファサードとガラス越しに見える共用部（写真：スティーブ・ホール © ヘドリッチ・ブレッシング）
Courtyard facade (photo: Steve Hall © Hedrich Blessing)

このプロジェクトは六甲山の麓における285ユニットの健常高齢者のためのものである。敷地はかつては傾斜地に開かれた20,000平方メートルの平坦な運動場であった。3階建てで10メートル以下の高さという建築制限の中で、1,000平方メートルにつき14ユニットの密度を達成することが設計条件であった。
建物は山麓での敷地の高低差を利用しながら、3つの中庭と2つの庭園を囲むように建てられている。またその配置は、入居者達が南からの日差しを受けられるように45度傾けられている。敷地の低い部分のビラ棟では、リゾートに見られるデザインを採用した。これらのビラ棟は面積も大きく贅沢なつくりをしており、そこには本館からブリッジを渡ってたどり着くことができる。棟ごとに20台分設けられた駐車スペースの合計は80台分となる。
来館者は敷地に残された木中を抜けて玄関前の広場へと到達する。受付ロビーからは大阪の市街地の風景を望むことができる。

The 285-unit independent living project is located in a prestigious mountainside community above Osaka, The 5 acre site had previously been a corporate sports field flattened with large retaining walls at the top and bottom of the site. The site has a 3-story, 10-meter height limit—an extremely challenging constraint given the client's need to achieve a unit density of 57 units per acre.

Re-terracing the site to take advantage of code provisions allowed for the development of a 6-story, 20-meter high building 'nestled' into the hillside. To achieve the unit density, BAR developed three enclosed courtyards and two open courtyards. Rotating the building 45 degrees allowed all units to be southfacing. Borrowing a concept from resort design, the firm designed three 'villas' at the bottom of the site. These 'villa' units are the largest, most luxurious and semi-detached yet accessible via covered pedestrian bridges. BAR's four-building design creatively met both the client's program of 80 parking spaces and a local restriction of 20 parking spaces per building.

Capitalizing on the site's natural context, one enters the site at the top of a hill and drives through s forested grove of trees giving the impression of a long drive into the secluded arrival courtyard. Upon entering the reception lobby, one gets a distant view of Osaka beyond.

Client: Half Century More Co., Ltd.
Master Designer: BAR Architects
Architect for Schematic Design: BAR Architects
Architect for Design Development: BAR Architects
Interior Designer: Babey Moulton Jue & Booth
Interior Designer for Skilled Nursing:
    Office of Dennis Cope/Architect
Landscape Designer: SWA Group
Predominant Contractor: Obayashi Corporation

Location: Takarazuka-shi, Hyogo Japan
Completion: 2005
Site Area: 12,000 sqm
Gross Floor Area: 26,500 sqm
Height: Under ground 1 story; Above ground 6 stories
Structure: Concrete structure
Number of Rooms: 285 rooms
Parking: 30 cars
Finishes:
<Predominant Exterior Wall>
    Tile and Stone
<Main lobby>
    Floor: Stone
    Wall: Wood and Fabric
    Ceiling: Gypsum Board

明るい色調のカジュアルダイニング（写真：スティーブ・ホール © ヘドリッチ・ブレッシング）
Casual dining (photo: Steve Hall © Hedrich Blessing)

プライベートダイニング （写真：スティーブ・ホール © ヘドリッチ・ブレッシング）
Private dining (photo: Steve Hall © Hedrich Blessing)

さりげない幾何学模様を用いたメイン・ダイニングルーム（写真：スティーブ・ホール © ヘドリッチ・ブレッシング）
Main dining room (photo: Steve Hall © Hedrich Blessing)

壁面装飾照明のあるラウンジ
（写真：スティーブ・ホール © ヘドリッチ・ブレッシング）
Lounge (photo: Steve Hall © Hedrich Blessing)

ゆったりとした空間のプロムナード（写真：スティーブ・ホール © ヘドリッチ・ブレッシング）
Promenade (photo: Steve Hall © Hedrich Blessing)

印象的なアプローチの先にある玄関廻りの夕景（写真：スティーブ・ホール © ヘドリッチ・ブレッシング）
Arrival court at sunset (photo: Steve Hall © Hedrich Blessing)

コートヤード側のファサード
（写真：スティーブ・ホール © ヘドリッチ・ブレッシング）
Courtyard facade (photo: Steve Hall © Hedrich Blessing)

テラス状に配された居住棟（写真：スティーブ・ホール © ヘドリッチ・ブレッシング）
Terraced residential buildings (photo: Steve Hall © Hedrich Blessing)

植栽が施されたガーデンコートヤード（写真：スティーブ・ホール © ヘドリッチ・ブレッシング）
Garden courtyard (photo: Steve Hall © Hedrich Blessing)

配置図
Site Plan

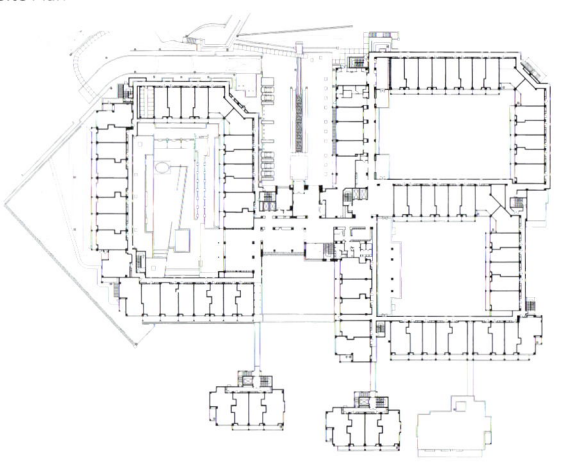

ロビー・居室階平面図
Lobby and residential units floor plan

幅の広いカウンターのあるバーダイニング
（写真：スティーブ・ホール © ヘドリッチ・ブレッシング）
Bar dining (photo: Steve Hall © Hedrich Blessing)

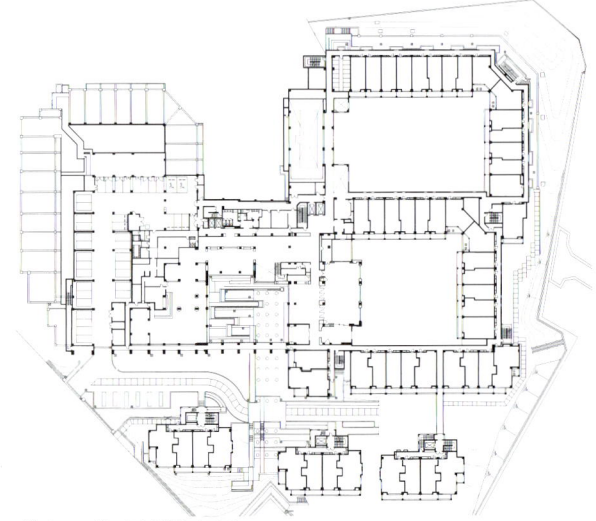

ダイニング・居室階平面図
Dining and residential units floor plan

居室平面図
Unit plan

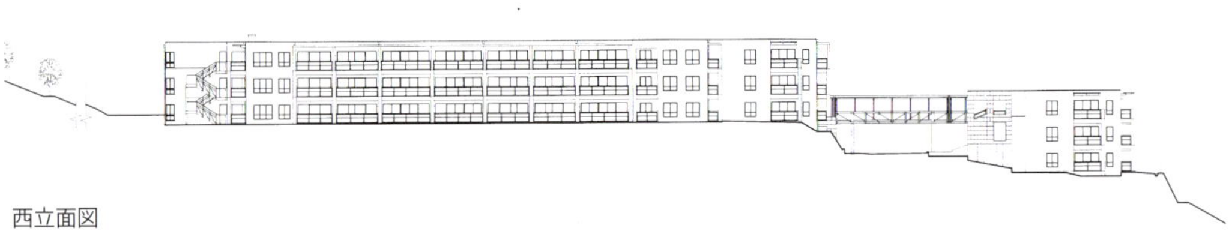

西立面図
West elevation

床にアクセントカラーを用いた居住棟の廊下
（写真：スティーブ・ホール ©ヘドリッチ・ブレッシング）
Residential corridor (photo: Steve Hall © Hedrich Blessing)

大き目のプライベート・ダイニング
（写真：スティーブ・ホール ©ヘドリッチ・ブレッシング）
Private dining (photo: Steve Hall © Hedrich Blessing)

大階段（写真：スティーブ・ホール ©ヘドリッチ・ブレッシング）
Grand stair (photo: Steve Hall © Hedrich Blessing)

いくつかのコーナーがあるライブラリー
（写真：スティーブ・ホール ©ヘドリッチ・ブレッシング）
Library (photo: Steve Hall © Hedrich Blessing)

Buckingham's Choice

バッキンガムズ・チョイス

山岳地域のパノラマを望む丘の頂きに悠然と展開するCCRC

A new continuing care retirement community on a 42-acre hilltop site with panoramic views of the Monocacy River.

メリーランド州のモノカシー渓谷と周囲の山岳のパノラマを望む160,000平方メートルの丘の頂きにある敷地に、パーキンス・イーストマンの設計によるこの新しいCCRCは展開する。のどかなこの地方のイメージを反映したこのコミュニティの設計では、自立性や選択性に富む介助施設と長期介護施設とを共用部と支援部門で統合している。

キャンパスは、137棟の健常者用コテージ、80戸の健常者用アパートメント、45室の介護付居住ユニット、42床の終身介護のスキルドナーシングベッドなどで構成されている。バッキンガムズ・チョイスは、フォーマルダイニングやカフェ、パブ、木工室、ビリヤード室、ダーツ・ポーカーゲーム室などのさまざまな共用施設、銀行、コンピュータセンター、プール付のヘルス・ウェルネスセンター、温室やコミュニティ庭園を有している。開放的な眺望と自然光による効果を強調するために、インテリアデザインには、淡く着色された木材と自然を喚起させるアクセントのある深みのある天然色を使用している。

介護ユニットの玄関（写真：チュック・コイ・フォトグラフィ）
Exterior Assisted Living Entrance (photo: Chuck Choi Photography)

航空写真（写真：チュック・コイ・フォトグラフィ）
Exterior Aerial (photo: Chuck Choi Photography)

Client: Buckingham's Choice, Inc.
Master Designer: Perkins Eastman
Architect for Schematic Design: Perkins Eastman
Architect for Design Development: Perkins Eastman
Interior Designer: Perkins Eastman
Landscape Designer: Graham Landscape Architecture
Predominant Contractor: Morgan-Keller, Inc.

Perkins Eastman designed this new continuing care retirement community on a 42-acre hilltop site with panoramic views of the Monocacy River Valley and surrounding mountains. The community's design reflects the imagery of its rural Maryland context, maximizes personal independence and choice, and integrates assisted living and long-term care accommodations with common and support facilities.

The campus includes 137 independent living cottages, 80 independent living apartments, 45 assisted living units, and 42 long-term care skilled nursing beds. In an effort to attract younger retirees and recognize the high percentage of couples living in the community, Buckingham's Choice offers diverse common facilities including formal dining; cafe and pub/Rathskeller; woodworking shop, billiards room and darts/poker game room; full-service bank; computer center; a health/wellness center with pool; and a greenhouse and community gardens. To enhance the open views and natural light, the interior design utilizes a rich combination of light stained woods and deep earth tones combined with nature-inspired accents.

パーラー（写真：チュック・コイ・フォトグラフィ）
Interior Parlor (photo: Chuck Choi Photography)

屋内プール（写真：チュック・コイ・フォトグラフィ）
Interior Pool (photo: Chuck Choi Photography)

Location: Adamstown, MD U.S.A.
Completion: 2000
Site Area: 160,000 sqm
Gross Floor Area: 39,020 sqm
Height: 3 stories
Structure:
    Cottages- Wood
    Main Building- Concrete Block, Roof Trusses
    Health Care Center- Load Bearing Metal
Number of Rooms: 255 rooms
Parking: 438 cars
Finishes:
<Predominant Exterior Wall>
    Vinyl Siding with Brick Accents
<Main lobby>
    Floor: Printed Cut Pile Carpet
    Wall: Vinyl Wall Covering
    Ceiling: Gypsum Wallboard
Award: Contemporary Long Term Care Order of Excellence/Outstanding Architectural and Interior Design, 2001 and the American Institute of Architects Design for Aging, 2002.

配置図
Site plan

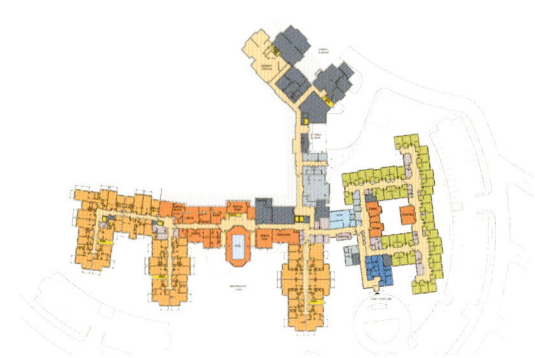

3階平面図
3rd floor plan

2階平面図
2nd floor plan

1階平面図
1st floor plan

第四章
大都市での利便性に恵まれた
都心回帰型

Chapter Four
Tokyo Experiment

The Barrington House Bajikoen

ザ・バーリントンハウス馬事公苑

歴史ある、四季の香り豊かな馬事公苑の地に映える英国貴族の別荘
English noble villa - Stately house at Bajikoen with historical and seasonal flavor.

英国伝統の様式を受け継ぐ品格ある外観
Exterior view incorporating tradition of gentle English style

英国伝統の様式美を受け継ぎ、貴族の別荘のような威風堂々たる佇まい、そして内装には現代的な洗練を融合させたクラシックコンテポラリー・スタイルを採用。エントランスホールなどの共用空間は、バックグラウンドミュージック、照明、小さな調度品に至るまで精選している。

家族や友人などのゲストを招くレジデンス（邸宅）は、木質をはじめとした素材の良さが生み出す品格に、収納の機能性も兼ね備えている。

共用施設では、その時の気分や用途によって選べるレストランが全部で5種類あり、日々の大きな楽しみであり健康の源でもある「食」を優雅に演出しているほか、クリニックやエステティック、フィットネスによる独自の新しいメディケアシステムが活きている。また趣味の充実のためのレクリエーションスペースやパーティーのための会場、ビジネスサロンなど、利用者の満足に近づけるよう日常の選択肢を取り揃えている。

サービスをコーディネートするコンシェルジュや身の回りの用事をつかさどるメイド、健康を見守るドクターやナース、将来の安心を支えるケアスタッフやケアマネージャーが居住者の生活をサポートしている。

英国貴族の別荘「ステートリーハウス」をイメージしたエントランスポーチ
Entrance poach designed to have sense of English noble villa - Stately house

Client: The Barrington House, Inc.
Master Designer: Comsn Inc. & Kenchiku Kikaku Sekkeisha
Architect for Schematic Design: Comsn Inc. & Kenchiku Kikaku Sekkeisha
Architect for Design Development: Comsn Inc. & Kenchiku Kikaku Sekkeisha
Interior Designer: Kenchiku Kikaku Sekkeisha
Landscape Designer: Hiroshi Ebisawa Architects & Associates
Predominant Contractor: Tokyu Construction Co., Ltd.

Featuring classic contemporary style, this facility combines nobility of authenticity in English tradition for exterior with sophisticated modern taste for interior. For public areas such as entrance hall, careful attention is paid in selection of background music, lighting fixture and miscellaneous display.
Residence with quality of wood and others is functionally designed to have storage to invite family or visitor.
Five dining rooms serve several ranges of food according to appetite or purpose of residents. Unique medical care system provides thorough clinic, aesthetic to fitness.
To support enriching hobby, we prepare recreation space, banquet room and business saloon for choice of guests for their satisfaction.
And to assist life, we distribute concierge and maids, doctor and nurse, and care staff and care manager.

ライブラリー
Library

メインダイニング
Main dining room

メディケアを核としたプール
Indoor pool serving medical care

ラウンジ
Lounge

ランドスケープ・コンセプト
Landscape concept

英国の伝統的スタイルの庭園
English style garden

使いやすさと美しさを兼ねそなえたダイニングキッチン
Dining kitchen with function and aesthetics

ダイニングキッチン
Dining kitchen

Location: Setagaya-ku, Tokyo Japan
Completion: 2006
Site Area: 7,792 sqm
Gross Floor Area: 17,576 sqm
Story: Under ground 1 story; Above ground 7 stories
Structure: Reinforced Concrete structure
Number of Room: 147 rooms
Parking: cars
Finishes:
<Predominant Exterior Wall>
        Stone and Tile
<Main lobby>
        Floor: Carpet
        Wall: Paint
        Ceiling: Paint

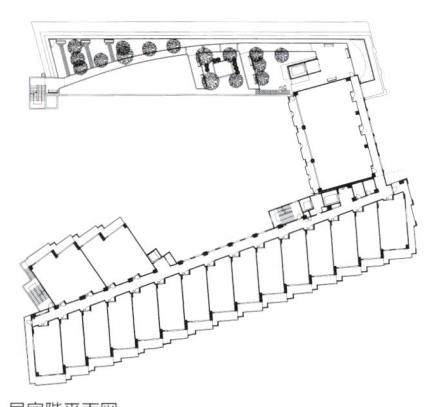

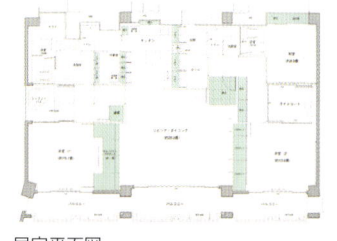

居室階平面図
Residents room floor plan

居室平面図
Unit plan

1階平面図
1st floor plan

居室のリビング
Living at resident room

居室
Resident room

Aria Ebisu
アリア恵比寿

都心で「くらす」ことへの一つの提案
Experiment of Urban-life in the heart of Tokyo.

木製ルーバーに包まれた外観
Exterior view enclosed by wood louver

アリア恵比寿という建物はその立地の特性上、「都心に住む（住みつづける）こと」への一つの提案かもしれない。周辺の景観を取り込み、限られた外部空間を有効に活用している。

前面道路と介護居室のバッファーとして設置した木製ルーバーは、内外をやわらかくルーズにつなげつつ周辺環境へのアクセントとして機能する。

建物の顔としてのエントランスは、外来者の応対に限らず、入居者の休憩の場所であったり、家族との面会の場所であったり、外部との接点として機能している。エントランス脇のエレベーターホールに配置した読書コーナーは入居者の書籍も持ち込まれ、利用頻度も高い活用の場所となっている。

ダイニングルームは地階ではあるが、外部の光庭(夜間は本当に光る)と一体的に計画して、閉塞感・圧迫感を解消している。また、家具レイアウトにバリエーションを作って食事のシチュエーションを変えることが出来るようにしている。

外部空間の活用として中庭は「見せる場所」「たたずむ場所」「触れる場所」として周辺の環境を取り込みつつ計画している。2階のウッドデッキではガーデニングセラピーや園芸療法も行われている。そこでは隣接する緑地の眺望を取り込み、入居者の憩いの場所としている。

「施設」のようなイメージを払拭し、入居者の「生活のステージ」として機能することを目標としている。

さまざまなシチュエーションに対応できるダイニングルーム
Dining room flexible for situation

Proposing "Living in Urban area (eternally)", the Ebisu Aria is located in the midst of urban context of Tokyo. Outdoor spaces of this facility introduce limited surrounding environment. Wooden louver enclosing facade as an accent within the adjacent environment and creating a buffer between street and resident rooms loosely connects inside with outside.

Entrance hall as a face of building has multi function: welcoming visitors, providing amenity with residents, meeting with family and connecting outside and inside. Library, located adjacent to elevator hall, stores books brought by residents and is one of the most popular spot for the resident.

Dinning room along with exterior light court, in spite of its underground location, extends view to outside to minimize feeling of blockage and pressure. Layout of furniture is flexible enough to suite variable setting of meals served in the room.

Courtyard introducing adjacent environment, one of the exterior areas of the building, is designed to be a place for to "watch", "stay" and "touch". A wood deck on the 2nd level introducing adjacent green and scenery provides gardening therapy and treatments and a place to venue.

Design of building tried to reducing image of "Institution" to attain creation of "Stage of Life" of the residents.

Client: Benesse Style Care Co., Ltd.
Master Designer: Benesse Style Care Co., Ltd.
Architect for Schematic Design: Shinichi Okada Architect & Associates
Architect for Design Development: Shinichi Okada Architect & Associates
Interior Designer: Takashimaya Space Create Co., Ltd.
Predominant Contractor: Tokyu Construction Co., Ltd.

光庭に面するダイニングルーム
Dining room extending to the light court

ロビー
Reception lobby

「老人ホーム」というと、とかく「施設」と言う認識をもたれがちである。しかし実際にホームの中で生活をする入居者にとって、ここは「いえ」であるべきだと思う。我々の展開する「ホーム」は「施設」ではなくて介護サービス等を中心にした「いえ」なのである。この中でこれまでの暮らしを続けたり、新しい暮らしの提案を行っている。

People tend to think "Retirement house" as "Institutional facility". But we believe that the place should be a "House" for residents. "Homes" we develop are not "Institutions" but "Houses" focusing on care services. We hope continuity of conventional life of the residents and propose new life style.

アルコーブのある個室
Resident room with alcove

Location: Meguro-ku, Tokyo JAPAN
Completion: 2005
Site Area: 1,313 sqm
Gross Floor Area: 2,784 sqm
Height: Under ground 1 story; Above ground 3 stories
Structure: Reinforce Concrete structure
Number of Rooms: 56 rooms
Parking: 7 cars
Finishes:
<Predominant Exterior Wall>
    Ceramics Tile and Exposed Concrete FUC
<Main lobby>
    Floor: Tile Carpet
    Wall: ARP
    Ceiling: ARP

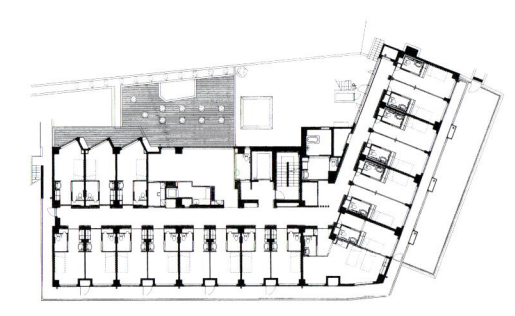

檜風呂
Hinoki bathing room

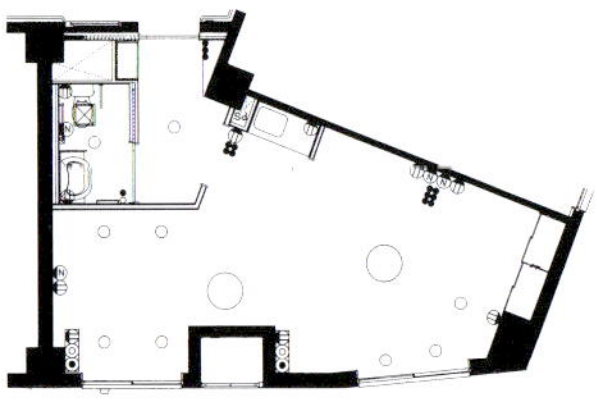

居室平面図
Unit plan

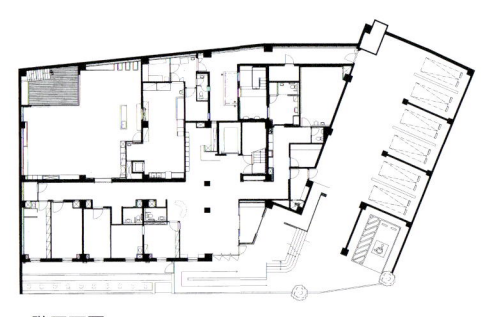

2階平面図
2nd floor plan

1階平面図
1st floor plan

明るい雰囲気のコミュニティルーム
Community room with natural light

バーカウンターのあるコミュニティルーム
Community room with bar counter

ライブラリーとしてのラウンジ
Lounge as library

Aria Bajikoen
アリア馬事公苑

住宅街に埋め込まれたガラスブロックの「いえ」
A "House" of glass block inserted in residential area.

ガラスブロックが特徴の外観
View from street featured by glass blocks

Client: Benesse Style Care Co., Ltd.
Master Designer: Benesse Style Care Co., Ltd.
Architect for Schematic Design: Shinichi Okada Architect & Associates
Architect for Design Development: Shinichi Okada Architect & Associates
Interior Designer: Takashimaya Space Create Co., Ltd.
Predominant Contractor: Matsumura-Gumi Corporation

うなぎの寝床状かつ緩やかな傾斜地にアリア馬事公苑は計画されている。有料老人ホームという特性から地階に介護居室を設けることが出来ないため、自然と地階の1フロアを共用部門、地上の3層を入居者の介護居室の部門と立体的に部門分けを行っている。

周辺環境との距離が取れない場合、室内環境の向上と外部環境の活用が大きなテーマとなるわけだが、ここでは窓前の自然や内部からのアイストップ、作業する事のできる外部環境というテーマを持って対応している。

エントランスは敷地の特性上奥の地階にあり、そのため視認性は自然と低くなる。外部(ここでは特に前面道路)との境界をガラスブロックで構成しファサードを作ることで建物としての存在感を出している。

エントランス正面に段状の花壇を配し、正面のアイストップとしている。エントランスホール脇の外部ラウンジと一体的に組み合わせることで、ダイニングの前室的な要素を持たせているため、普段外部に出る事の少ない入居者にとって「ソト」・「シキ」・「シゼン」を感じる要素となっている。

各階の共用部(ラウンジ)の平面形状に変化をつけることで、階別に認識しやすくすると同時に各階の特徴を持たせている。認知症優先フロアの共用部は見通しのよい空間とし、スタッフの見守りも強化している。また、装飾品は昭和をイメージした、懐かしい雰囲気の中でくつろげるスペースとしている。屋上庭園を園芸コーナーとすることで、利用者が実際に作業できるスペースを確保している。

The Aria Bajikoen suites on its eel like unique configuration of site with gentle slope. Since resident rooms should not be underground level, design team allocated public area on the 1st level underground and resident area on three levels above ground.

Such site without enough distance from adjacent must have solution to improve indoor environment and utilize outdoor environment. As specific solutions we prepared natural environment in front of window, eye stop from inside and outdoor space for activities.

Since entrance is set back from street and located underground level according to characteristics of site, it is not clearly recognized. Enclosing a facade on a predominant street by glass blocks makes appearance of this building unique.

A series of stepping flower boxes in front of entrance stops sight of visitors. Combination of the flower boxes with an outdoor lounge side of entrance hall, as an antechamber of dining, creates feeling of "Outside", "Season" and "Nature" residents who seldom go out.

Plans of lounge on each level differ to create specific characteristics and sense of recognition of places. Public areas for predominantly dementia have clear view and comprehensive observation by staff. To provide comfortable space with nostalgia, fixture imaging era of Showa are distributed. Roof garden provides opportunity residents to enjoy gardening.

快適なコミュニティルーム
Comfortable community room

四季を感じる屋外デッキ
Outdoor deck with feeling of season

Location: Setagaya-ku, Tokyo JAPAN
Completion: 2005
Site Area: 1,480 sqm
Gross Floor Area: 2,573 sqm
Height: Under ground 1 story; Above ground 3 stories
Structure: Reinforced Concrete structure
Number of Rooms: 46 rooms
Parking :6 cars
Finishes:
<Predominant Exterior Wall>
    Ceramics Tile and Exposed Concrete
<Main lobby>
    Floor: Wood and Sandstone
    Wall: Vinyl Wall Covering and Limestone
    Ceiling: Vinyl Wall Covering

屋外デッキに接するダイニングルーム
Dining room adjacent to outdoor deck

1 階平面図
1st floor plan

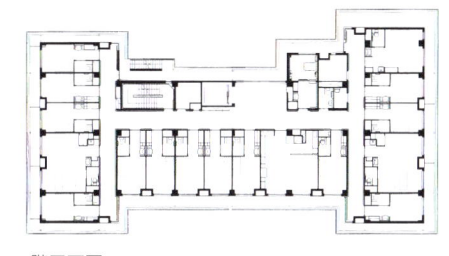

3 階平面図
3rd floor plan

Comsn Garden Sakurashinmachi
コムスンガーデン桜新町

潤いに満ちた日々を育む特等席
Special place enriching daily life.

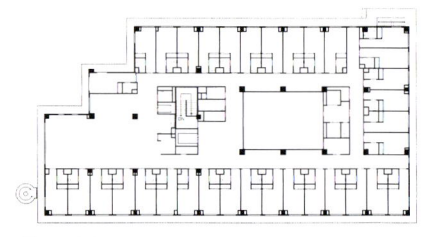

1階平面図
1st floor plan

Location: Setagaya-ku, Tokyo Japan
Completion: 2005
Site Area: 2,559 sqm
Gross Floor Area: 3,752 sqm
Height: 3 stories
Structure: Reinforced Concrete structure
Number of Rooms: 82 rooms
Parking: 7 cars
Finishes:
<Predominant Exterior Wall>
　　　Ceramic Tile
<Main lobby>
　　　Floor: Carpet
　　　Wall: Marble Stone
　　　Ceiling: Wall Covering

品格を漂わせる風情豊かな竹林にかこまれた外観
Facade with gentle manner with bamboo trees

Client: Comsn Inc.
Master Designer: Comsn, Inc.
Architect for Schematic Design: Comsn Inc.
Architect for Design Development: Tokyu Construction Co., Ltd.
Predominant Contractor: Tokyu Construction Co., Ltd.

明るい中庭を配置し、共用部への採光を考慮していることが特徴である。これによって施設全体が明るい雰囲気となるばかりか、中庭に面する浴室の上に配された空中庭園をさまざまな角度から楽しむことができるようになっている。また、都心では建物の周囲に十分な広さの庭の確保が難しいため、屋上庭園でこれを補っている。

A courtyard lit with natural sunlight contributes creation of bright environment of this facility. From various locations in the facility, residents enjoy watching the charming sky garden designed on a roof of the sammunal bathing. A roof garden on the top of the building solve problem of difficulty to allocate garden on the surface in the site located in urban area.

思い思いのカルチャーライフを楽しめるラウンジ
Lounge to experience variable cultural life

Comsn Garden Yoganomori
コムスンガーデン用賀の杜

涼風と緑豊かな高台で、豊かな寛ぎの時を刻む住空間
Residence with sense of comfortable time on the top of hill, in breeze and green.

Location: Setagaya-ku, Tokyo Japan
Completion: 2005
Site Area: 6,094 sqm
Gross Floor Area: 6,062 sqm
Height: 3 stories
Structure: Reinforced Concrete structure
Number of Rooms: 123 rooms
Parking: 22 cars
Finishes:
<Predominant Exterior Wall>
　　　Ceramic Tile
<Main lobby>
　　　Floor: Carpet
　　　Wall: Wall Covering
　　　Ceiling: Wall Covering

エントランスポーチ
Entrance poach

Client: Comsn Inc.
Master Designer: Comsn Inc.
Architect for Schematic Design: Toda Corporation
Architect for Design Development: Toda Corporation
Predominant Contractor: Toda Corporation

2階まで吹き抜けの気持ちのよいリビング
Living with comfortable atrium

敷地が広く高台にあり、周囲に高い建物も無い事から広がりのある建物配置を実現した。建物をH型にする事で、2つの中庭を設け全ての居室から日差しを感じ、緑を眺められるよう配慮した。居室とリビングの配置はフロアーごとにもサービスが提供できる広さがあり、リビングダイニングからは南面の光豊かな中庭と北面の緑豊かな坪庭を楽しむことができる。1階リビングには開放感のある吹き抜けを設け、中庭に面する壁はカーテンウォールを用いてさらに開放感を向上させている。また、外部利用者も考慮したクリニックやフィットネスルームも完備する他、スタッフのスペースを広めに確保している。

Since hilly location with view to surrounding area, configuration of building has a sense of spacious. H shape of plan with two courtyards attains all resident rooms to have sunlight and view to green outside. Services for resident rooms and common living area are provided through a floor by a floor bases. From the living-dining residents enjoy view to the south courtyard with sunlight and north small courtyard with abundant green. The atrium at living room on the 1st floor extends to outside through the curtain wall facing the courtyard. Clinic and fitness are available for also visitors, and large enough spaces are prepared for staff.

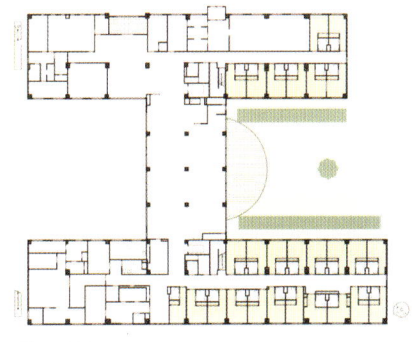

1階平面図
1st floor plan

Charming Square Shirogane

チャーミングスクエア白金

東京の中心部に建つ高層高齢者コミュニティ
Independent Living Facility with 129 Luxury Apartments, Assisted Living: 23 Apartments, Dementia Care: 8 Units in the heart of Tokyo.

ロトンダと暖炉脇のラウンジ（レンダリング：3rd スペースデザイン）
Rotunda and Fireside Lounge (rendering: 3rd Space Design)

東京の中心部でのこの10階建ての高齢者コミュニティは、160戸のアパートメントや介護施設、認知症介護施設、玄関ホールや5つ星のレストラン、カラオケやゲーム室、マージャン室、シアター、ビューティーサロン、大浴場、アスレチックジム、ウェルネスセンター、リハビリテーションエリアなどからなる。設計には西洋のデザインと日本の伝統的なデザインの融合が求められた。

認知症介護のプログラムづくりでは、日米の設計チームが共にユニットのレイアウトを検討し、またサイン計画では米国にあるような特徴あるデザインを多く適用した。全般的には安全面と管理面に配慮しながら、居住者の尊厳と自立を促そうとするデザインとなっている。

This ten story, retirement community in the heart of Tokyo will consist of 160 apartments, assisted living, dementia care and Commons area, including entrance hall, 5-star restaurant, karaoke rooms, game room, mah-jongg room, theater, art center, library, beauty salon, communal bathing, athletic gym, wellness center and rehabilitation areas. Our firm was asked to create an international design that incorporates Western design and traditional Japanese design.

Merlino Design Partnership is proud of our influence in shaping the Dementia Care program for Charming Square Shirogane. Together with our Japanese counterparts, we have created a new physical layout for the unit and implemented many of the design features, visual queuing and way finding techniques that are used in the USA. Our design will maximize the residents dignity and independence while maintaining safety and control.

Restaurant looking through water feature (rendering: 3rd Space Design)

Project Team
Client: ZECS, Co.
Architect for Schematic Design: Kura Architects & Engineers, Inc.
Architect for Design Development:
	Merlino Design Partnership, Inc.
	with Affiliate Firm: KD Associates, PA
Interior Designer: Merlino Design Partnership, Inc.
Interpreting & Communications: Mr. Shigenobu Ueoka, ICSI, Inc.
Predominant Contractor: Taisei Corporation, Tokyo Branch

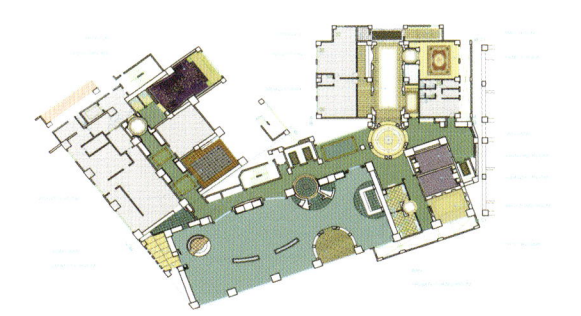

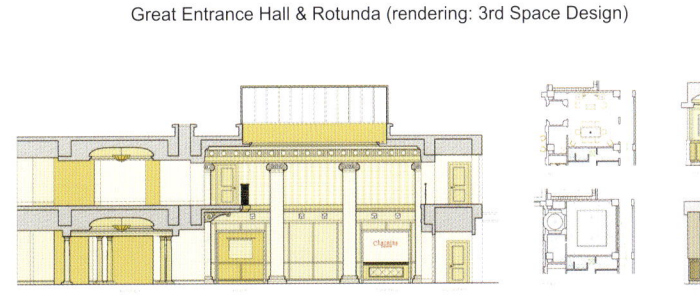

Great Entrance Hall & Rotunda (rendering: 3rd Space Design)

from left: First Floor Color Coded Floor Plan, Great Hall North Elevation, Family Room with Commissioned Mural (drawing: Merlino Design Partnership)

Location: Minato-Ku, Tokyo Japan
Completion: 2008
Site Area: 5,196 sqm
Gross Floor Area: 18,765 sqm
Height: Under ground 2 stories; Above ground 10 stories
Structure: Steel Reinforced Concrete structure
Number of Rooms: 160 apartments
Parking: 39 underground
Finishes:
<Predominant Exterior Wall>
	First/Second Floor: Granite, Three thru Ten: Tile
<Main lobby>
	Floor: Marble Tile with Custom Area Rugs
	Wall: Wallboard with Milled Walls with Ornamental Trim
	Ceiling: Plaster Ceiling with Ornamental Trim

Front Entrance with Porte Cochere (rendering: Kura Architects)

Sun City Ginza East
サンシティ銀座・イースト

東京の都心、「銀座」における超高層CCRC
One of Japan's first urban high-rise continuing care retirement communities (CCRC's) in Tokyo.

建物頂部
Exterior Crown

東京の都心にある高齢者コミュニティである32階建のサンシティ銀座・イーストは、日本ではめずらしい超高層CCRCである。この施設は、東京や大阪の都心部でハイスタンダードな施設を展開する事業者であり、日本でのシニアケア施設づくりの分野では最先端をゆくハーフ・センチュリー・モアによるものである。

6層のポディウムの上に26層を加えた延べ床面積39,668平方メートルのこの施設の建設費は92億円である。ポディウムは通りに面した2層の共用部と134室のナーシングユニットからなる。ベースの端部での2層や3層の吹き抜けによってダイナミックな表情となっているばかりか、さまざまな居住環境が関連付けられている。吹き抜けのあるハーバービュー・レストランや銀座バーがある最上階までの23層には276室の健常者用住戸がある。ここでは居住階での可能な限りの眺望を得ることが主要な目的の一つであった。3つの長方形をずらして平面を構成することで、住戸はコーナービューを得ることができ、スリムなプロポーションと適度なスケール感のあるタワーとなった。住戸からの眺望を大きく確保するための構造のありかたや、東京のスカイラインに映える建物となるように配慮した。

インテリアデザインでは、洗練されたライフスタイルを求める居住者の嗜好を反映した。上品な雰囲気を出すために、贅沢な仕上げや繊細なディテールが使われた。共用部のドラマティックで彫刻的な要素は、エキサイティングでエネルギーのあふれる東京そのものを表している。

水を使ったランドスケープ・アーキテクチュアでは、隅田川や南側の運河からヒントを得ている。このキャンパスの特徴である滝と流れは、北側の広場を源とし、建物の西側のファサードに沿った黒御影石の水路へと導かれて南に向かう。張り巡らされた庭やプラザはさまざまな屋外での楽しみを提供し、このシニアコミュニティのランドマークの共用部分に潤いを与えている。

Sun City Ginza East, a 32-story retirement community in downtown Tokyo, is one of Japan's first urban high-rise CCRCs. The development of this project marks a significant commitment by Half Century More, a leader in Japan's senior care revolution, to bring the same high standards of design and care, found in their Tokyo and Osaka facilities, into the heart of the city.

The $80 million, 39,668 sqm building is organized around a six-story podium base capped by a 26-floor tower. The podium is made up of two levels of public space at the street, with 134 units of nursing-specific floors above. Double- and triple- height spaces at either end of the base provide a dynamic street presence and tie together the living environments. The tower offers 276 independent living apartments on 23 floors, capped by the two-story Harborview Restaurant and Ginza Bar.

An important goal for the residential floors was to develop a plan that offers as many view opportunities as possible. By aligning the floor plate as three shifted rectangles, each suite gains corner views and the tower itself achieves a slimmer proportion and a more graceful residential scale. The tower's structure was positioned to allow open corners in each apartment, thereby enhancing each apartment's view. Careful attention to designing the building's crown creates a building that enhances Tokyo's skyline.

The interior design goal was to design spaces that reflect the tastes of future residents seeking an upscale, sophisticated lifestyle. Through the use of a luxurious, yet restrained choice of materials and thoughtful attention to details, the project creates an atmosphere appropriate to the facility's clientele. Dramatic sculptural elements in the multi-storied public spaces are intended to evoke the excitement and energy of Tokyo itself.

The landscape architecture promotes the use of water throughout the site, taking its cue from the Sumida River to the west and the man-made boat channel immediately to the south. The campus features a waterfall and stream that originates in the north plaza, is directed into a black granite water channel that continues along the building's west facade and terminates in a linear slot at the south, which suggests connection to the boat canal beyond. Woven throughout are gardens and plazas that provide a variety of outdoor experiences, and complement and activate the public spaces of this landmark senior community.

Client: Half Century More Co., Ltd.
Master Designer: Perkins Eastman
Architect for Schematic Design: Perkins Eastman
Architect for Design Development:
   Perkins Eastman
   Nikken Housing Systems Ltd. (architectural consultant)
Interior Designer: Barry Design Associates
Landscape Designer: SWA Group
Predominant Contractor: Shimizu Corporation

全景
Exterior Overall

正面玄関廻り
Exterior Entry

玄関庇
Exterior Canopy

ダイニング
Dining

Location: Chuo-ku, Tokyo Japan
Completion: 2006
Site Area: 5,600 sqm
Gross Floor Area: 39,668 sqm
Height: Under ground 1 story; Above ground 31 stories
Structure: Concrete with steel structure
Number of Rooms: 410 rooms
Parking: 140 underground mechanical parking
Finishes:
<Predominant Exterior Wall>
　　　Tile with Aluminum Trim
<Main lobby>
　　　Floor: Various Stone Tile
　　　Wall: Various Paneling
　　　Ceiling: Vinyl Wall Covering and Wood Trim

ライブラリー
（レンダリング：ボブ・カミンスキー）
Library (Rendering: Bob Kaminski)

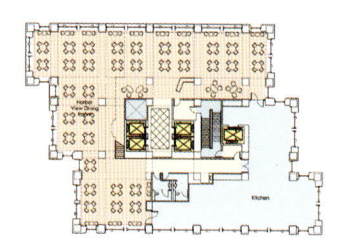

31階平面図
31st floor plan

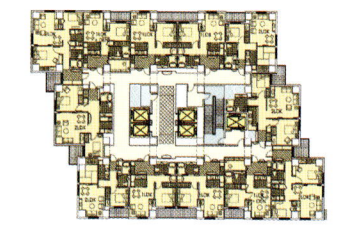

8-30階平面図
8th - 30th floor plan

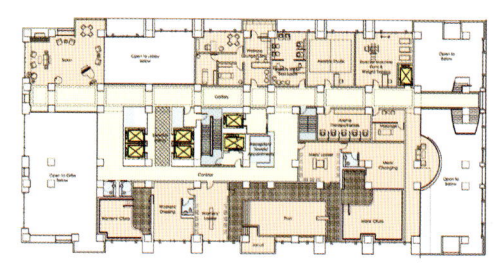

2階平面図
2nd floor plan

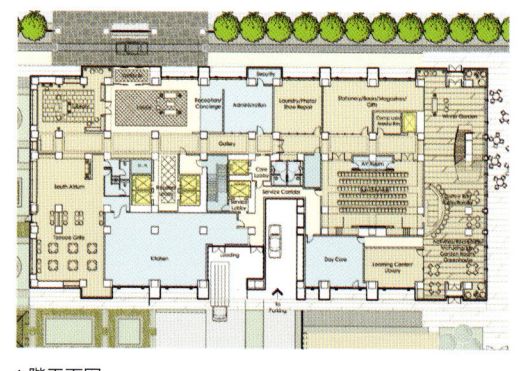

1階平面図
1st floor plan

謝辞
Ackowledgments

グラフィック社の大田悟氏から本書編纂の誘いを受けたのが平成17年5月であった。我が国の高齢者を巡る社会整備が今後ますます活況を呈する中で、国内外のアッパーミドルからハイエンドレベルにいたる居住施設に焦点をあてた本を作りたいとのことであった。私が外資系建築設計事務所に在籍中に、高齢者施設の建設にかかわっていたことを知っての上でである。

その後、この分野では先行する米国での事情を知ろうと、在日米国大使館商務部の大村泰蔵氏や、豊富な設計経験を有するデニス・コープ氏ならびに国内では笹美香氏等からの助言を得ながら、膨大な量の候補の中から取材すべき対象を絞り込んだ。本書で紹介した施設以外にも優れた運営を行う施設は豊富にあるものの、ここではその取り組みがデザインの質の高さとして具現化されているものを対象とした。

取材を通して、エンドユーザー（入居高齢者）の多様なニーズを分析しそれに適確に応えようとする事業者のアプローチの特異性や、とりわけ建築家やデザイナーの質がその施設に反映されていることが判った。また本書での章立ては、従来の制度的類型によるものにとらわれずに、むしろそこでの革新的なプログラムへの取り組みや、戦略的更新、地域性への依拠、都心での展開といった観点からの分類によって成り立っている。

なお本書は多くの方々の理解と協力を得られたことによって刊行に至ることができた。事業者であるグッドウィル・グループ㈱の生井伸一氏、コベルコビジネス

In May 2005, Satoru Ota of Graphic-sha Publishing Co., Ltd commissioned me to edit this book. Prior to the commission he had known of my experience with local projects for senior living from my work at a foreign architectural firm in Tokyo. After being commissioned by Satoru Ota, I consulted with Taizo Omura - Commercial Attaché of Embassy of the United State of America in Japan, Dennis Cope - my senior colleague at the firm, and Mika Sasa - an expert in this field, to establish the editorial policy of the book and develop a list of potential contributors to be chosen for this book from among the considerable number of candidates.

Through analysis of project descriptions, photos and drawings prepared by the contributors to the book, the editorial team identified those developers and architects who are leaders in creating places of quality that address the various special needs of senior residents. The team then synthesized these into the four categories -chapters- of the book.

I appreciate the clients who deeply understood the concept of this book: The Applied Companies, BAC Associates, Bridgepoint Assisted Living, Buckingham's Choice, Inc., Classic Residence by Hyatt, Front Porch, Gemeindeverband Neumarkt am Wallersee, Givens Estates, Hamilton Avenue Properties, Jewish Home for Aged, Life Enriching Communities, The Presbyterian Homes, Inc., Marilyn and Stanley M. Katz Seniors Campus, New England Deaconess Association, Seashore Gardens, Atlantic City, Senior Resource Group, LLC, Sozialhilfeverb and Leibnits, United Methodist Retirement Communities, and other qualified local developers.

Gratitude is also due to the architects/designers for their

サポート㈱の小山雅弘氏、㈱コムスンの市川広美氏・入江康文氏・佐藤泰氏・瀧本功氏、神鋼ケアライフ㈱の山下信行氏・見市拓氏、ディアージュ神戸の赤尾和也氏・朝倉和則氏・西谷伸二氏、㈱ハーフ・センチュリー・モアの稲村一志氏、福岡地所シニアライフ㈱の日高康志氏、㈱プライムステージの田部井弘氏・山崎忠男氏、㈱ベネッセスタイルケアの大倉園子氏・岡田仁氏・奥理恵子氏・横井祐子氏・米須正明氏、菱明ロイヤルライフ㈱の岩波美津江氏・武石徹氏・谷山裕治氏・堤公子氏、財団法人結核予防会、㈱ゼクス等に、ならびに取材に熱心に応じていただいた、㈱大林組の桜井則雄氏・安原光幸氏、鹿島の大越英俊氏・鈴木浩史氏・鈴木忠夫氏・藤田雄三氏、㈱久米設計の岡田良二氏・児玉耕二氏、スタジオヴォイドの金原孝興氏、㈱竹中工務店の森康郎氏や、写真家の小林浩志氏、杉野圭氏、中島悠二氏、濱田一郎氏、古川泰造氏、松岡満男氏、松田哲也氏等に、そして施設の紹介へと惜しみなく導いてくださった、コロンビア大学同窓生の片岡晃氏・香西元氏、㈱サン・ライフの津田佳志氏、森ビル㈱の本耕一氏等に、また国際関係の促進をしてくださった重盛ひろみ氏、中村眞澄氏に、この場を借りて深くお礼を申し上げます。

最後に編集を終えて本書が、個性豊かな居住者にとってより良い生活の拠りどころとなり、また事業者にとってもより戦略性に富んだ、今後の施設の展開に資することができれば幸いである。

平成18年9月
上利益弘

kind efforts with the preparation materials for the book: Linda Crouse, Doug Dun and Sherri Taylor at BAR Architects, Amy Jones and Tim Mueller at FreemanWhite, Inc., Alan Bright at HOK Group Inc., Bruce Hurowitz at Merlino Design Partnership, Inc., Brad Fanta, Leslie G. Moldow and Naoe White at Mithun, Dennis Cope at Office of Dennis Cope/Architect, Kilian Kada and Klaus Kada at Office Graz Klaus Kada, Penny Heinnickel, Sarah Mechling, Lori Miller and Jennifer Ray at Perkins Eastman Architects, Carlos Alfonso Gonzalez, Christina Monti and Dora Ng at Steinberg Architects, Constantine L. Tsomides and Sarah J. Zarum at Tsomides Associates Architects Planners, Gerhard Wittfeld, and other respectful local architects/contractors.

And the photographers who supported this book considerably by permitting the inclusion of their photos are: Brad Anderson, Dennis Anderson, Applied Companies, Architectural Photography, Inc., Jaime Ardiles-Arce, Tom Bernard Photography, Bonjour Studios, Tim Buchman, Benny Chan, Chuck Choi Photography, Frank Constantino, Jerry Davis, Feinknopf Photography, Bob Golden Photography, Steve Hall, Timothy Hursley, Hutchins Photography, Angelo Kaunat, Massery Photography, Jason Meyer, Rion Rizzo, Billy Simcox, Margherita Spiluttini, and other professional local photographers.

Lastly, my wish with this book is to contribute to the further creation of better places for senior citizens as well as the strategic development of new facilities for clients.

Masuhiro Agari Int'l Assoc. AIA, JIA
September 2006

照会先
References

ARCHITEKTURBURO KADA
Univ. Prof. Arch. Di Klaus Kada
Wickenburggasse 32, Graz, Styria
Austria
www.kada-aachen.de

BAR Architects
543 Howard Street
San Francisco, CA 94105
U.S.A.
www.bararch.com

Benesse Style Care Co., Ltd.
Shibuya Higashiguchi Building 2F
2-22-3, Shibuya
Shibuya-ku, Tokyo 150-0002
Japan
株式会社ベネッセスタイルケア
東京都渋谷区渋谷 2-22-3
渋谷東口ビル 2 階
www.benesse-style-care.co.jp

COMSN, Inc.
Roppoingi Hills Mori Tower 35F
6-10-1, Roppongi
Minato-ku, Tokyo 106-6135
Japan
株式会社コムスン
東京都港区六本木 6-10-1
六本木ヒルズ森タワー 35F
www.comsn.com

FreemanWhite, Inc.
8025 Arrowridge Blvd.
Charlotte, NC 28273
U.S.A.
www.freemanwhite.com

Fukuoka Jisho Seniorlife Co., Ltd.
3-2-1, Kashiihama
Higashi-ku, Fukuoka 813-0016
Japan
福岡地所シニアライフ株式会社
福岡市東区香椎浜 3 丁目 2 番 1 号
www.will-mark.com

Half Century More Co., Ltd.
ARK Mori Building 30F
1-12-32, Akasaka
Minato-ku, Tokyo 107-6030
Japan
株式会社ハーフ・センチュリー・モア
東京都港区赤坂 1-12-32
www.hcm-suncity.jp

Hellmuth, Obata & Kassabaum (HOK)
One Bush Street - Suite 200
San Francisco, CA 94104
U.S.A.
www.hok.com

Kada-Wittfeld Architektur
THEATERSTRASSE 19
AACHEN, NRW 52062
Germany
www.kada-aachen.de

KAJIMA CORPORATION
Architectural Design Division
(KAJIMA DESIGN)
6-5-30, Akasaka
Minato-ku, Tokyo 107-8502
Japan
鹿島建設株式会社
建築設計本部
東京都港区赤坂 6-5-30
www.kajima.co.jp
www.kajima.co.jp/tech/kd

Kinki Ryoju Estate Co., Ltd.
9-2-19, Kasamatsudori
Hyogo-ku, Kobe 652-0864
Japan
近畿菱重興産株式会社
神戸市兵庫区笠松通 9-2-19
http://www.ryohkoh.co.jp
http://www.diage-kobe.com

Kumesekkei Co., ltd.
2-1-22, Shiomi
Koto-ku, Tokyo 135-8567
Japan
株式会社久米設計
東京都江東区潮見 2-1-22
www.kumesekkei.co.jp

MERLINO DESIGN PARTNERSHIP, INC.
2200 Renaissance Blvd, Suite 300
Gulph Mills, PA 19406
U.S.A.
www.MerlinoDesign.com

Mithun
1201 Alaskan Way, Suite 200
Seattle, WA 98101
U.S.A.
www.mithun.com

Mori Building Co., Ltd.
Roppongi Hills Mori Tower P.O. BOX 1
6-10-1, Roppongi
Minato-ku, Tokyo 106-6155
Japan
森ビル株式会社
東京都港区六本木 6-10-1
六本木ヒルズ森タワー私書箱 1 号
www.mori.co.jp

Obayashi Coporation
4-33 Kitahama-Higashi
Chuo-ku, Osaka 540-8584
Japan
株式会社大林組本店
大阪市中央区北浜東 4-33
www.obayashi.co.jp

Office of Dennis Cope/Architect
16408 NE 44th Way
Redmond, WA 98052
U.S.A.
www3.kcn.ne.jp/~odc-a/

Perkins Eastman
1100 Liberty Avenue
Pittsburgh, PA 15222
U.S.A.
www.perkinseastman.com

Primestage Co., Ltd.
8-22-1, Seijo
Setagaya-ku, Tokyo 157-8566
Japan
株式会社プラムステージ
東京都世田谷区成城 8-22-1
www.sacravia.co.jp

Ryomei Royal Life Co., Ltd.
1461 Shimooyamada-cho
Machida-shi, Tokyo 194-0202
Japan
菱明ロイヤルライフ株式会社
東京都町田市下小山田町 1461
www.royal-tama.co.jp

SHINKO CARE LIFE CO.,LTD
1-5-1, Wakinohamakaigandori
Cyuo-ku, Kobe 651-0073
Japan
神鋼ケアライフ株式会社
神戸市中央区脇浜海岸通 1-5-1
www.s-carelife.co.jp

Steinberg Architects
60 Pierce Ave
San Jose, CA 95110
U.S.A.
www.steinbergarchitects.com

Studio Void
1454-8-403. Mikageshironomae
Mikage-cho
Hgashi Nada-ku, Kobe 658-0056
Japan
スタジオ ヴォイド
神戸市東灘区御影町御影城ノ前 1454-8-403
www.studiovoid.com

Takenaka Corporation Osaka Office
4-1-13, Honmachi
Chuou-ku, Osaka 541-0053
Japan
株式会社竹中工務店大阪本店
大阪市中央区本町 4-1-13
www.takenaka.co.jp

Tsomides Associates Architects Planners/
TAAP
389 Elliot Street
Newton Upper Falls, MA 02464
U.S.A.
www.tsomides.com

上利益弘

東京都生まれ。日本大学大学院講師、文化庁派遣芸術家在外研修員（昭和63年度）、日本建築家協会登録建築家、米国建築家協会国際会員。日本大学を卒業の後、コロンビア大学大学院を修了。INA新建築研究所やアイゼンマン建築事務所、ヘルムス・オバタ・カッサバウム（HOK）建築事務所での実務を経て、現在、一級建築士事務所アガリ・アソシエイツ代表。建築・インテリアデザイン、国際プロジェクト・マネージメントなどの分野で活動を行う。デザイン・コンクール入選多数。

Masuhiro Agari, Int'l Assoc. AIA, JIA
B.E., Nihon University, 1980; M.S., in Advanced Architectural Design, Columbia University, 1997. Research fellowship, Ministry of Cultural Affairs/National Endowment for the Arts, 1988. Adjunct Associate Professor, Graduate School of Architecture, Nihon University. Registered Architect.

www.agari.net

企画
Directing Manager
大田　悟（グラフィック社）
Satoru Ohta (Graphic-sha)

エディトリアル・ディレクター
Editorial Director
上利　益弘
Masuhiro Agari

エディトリアル・アドバイザー
Editorial Advisor
デニス・コープ
Dennis Cope

取材協力
Co-Int'l Coordinator
中村　眞澄
Masumi Nakamura

デザイン協力
Co-Designer
中島　悠二
Yuji Nakajima

翻訳協力
Co-Translator
重盛　ひろみ
Hiromi Shigemori

校閲
Proofread
関　容子
Yoko Seki

Photographers for acket
　　Benny Chan (front)
　　Doug Dun (back)
　　Massery Photography (sleeve)

世界のシニアリビング

発行	2006年10月25日　初版第1刷発行
編纂	上利益弘©
発行者	久世利郎
発行所	株式会社グラフィック社 〒102-0073 東京都千代田区九段北1-14-17 Tel: 03-3263-4318／Fax: 03-3263-5297 郵便振替：00130-6-114345 http://www.graphicsha.co.jp

印刷・製本　錦明印刷株式会社

©2006 本書の内容は、著作権上の保護を受けています。著作権者及び出版社の文書による事前の同意を得ずに、本書の内容の一部、あるいは全部を無断で複写複製、転載することは禁じられています。

本書の内容における電話での質問はお受けできません。

乱丁・落丁はお取り替えいたします。

ISBN4-7661-1738-7　C3052